JESUS
WHO IS THIS
MAN
WHO SAYS HE'S
GOD?

To: "Dad"
From; Teresa, Blair
Danielle + Connor
12-25-04

JESUS

WHO IS THIS
MAN
WHO SAYS HE'S
GOD?

JESUS: *Who Is This Man Who Says He's God?*
© 2004 RBC Ministries

Discovery House Publishers is affiliated with
RBC Ministries, Grand Rapids, Michigan 49512

Cover Design: Stan Myers

Printed in the United States of America
04 05 06 07 08 09 / DP / 10 9 8 7 6 5 4 3 2 1

Contents

Preface

For 2,000 years, His name has been at the heart of worship and at the center of controversy. His life and work have been extolled in books, poetry, music, and film. His words have been scrutinized and vilified, and His message has been trusted by untold millions and rejected by scores of others. Still, for most people Jesus Christ remains a mystery.

Who was He really? What were His claims? What was His mission? Are those things true? These are the questions upon which eternity is hinged. Considering the person and work of Christ is a daunting challenge, yet it is a journey that is well worth the effort—and this journey begins with the decision and desire to know Him.

For that reason, in this volume, we have collected Bible teaching from four booklets out of RBC's popular Discovery Series. These particular booklets offer insight and encouragement to readers who want to more personally know and embrace the Savior, Jesus Christ. Our desire is that this collection will draw you ever closer to Him, and deepen your love for and relationship with Christ. May your heart be enriched as you embrace the Savior.

Bill Crowder
RBC Director of Church Ministries

1

The Amazing
Prophecy Of Names

During World War II, my father-in-law spent 18 months in a prisoner-of-war camp. In the camp, loudspeakers often played music, and one of the songs that was heard repeatedly was "Lili Marlene." Somehow it gave him hope, and he fell in love with the beauty of that name. Years later he gave that name, which was filled with personal significance, to his only daughter—my wife Marlene.

Names are like that. They have great importance in human relationships. Nowhere, however, is a name more important than in our relationship with the living Lord. In a way that sets Him apart from all others, He ties His name to His reputation, and then to His own self-introduction as "God with us."

This booklet is about the amazing prophecy of Isaiah 9:6, where the prophet, 700 years before the coming of Messiah, described the One whose names reveal His importance to us.

Bill Crowder

What's In A Name?

What's in a name? Shakespeare's *Romeo And Juliet* made this question famous. They fall in love before learning they bear the names of rival families. Romeo is a Montague and Juliet a Capulet. Willing to deny name before love, Juliet cries out, "Romeo, Romeo! Wherefore art thou, Romeo? Deny thy father and refuse thy name. Or if thou wilt not, be but sworn my love, and I'll no longer be a Capulet." A few lines later, Juliet asks, "What's in a name? That which we call a rose, by any other name would smell as sweet."

In other settings, the family name can seem more important. I remember as a young boy watching my father go through the pain of a failed business that left my parents several thousand dollars in debt. Rather than declare bankruptcy, he went to each of his creditors and told them he would pay them back every cent if it took him until the day he died. On his handshake and his name, each creditor took him at his word—and he kept his promise to the full, furthering his credibility and testimony of integrity in the business community.

A name is important. From the day of our birth, our parents use our name to link us to their own preferences and values. People name their sons Peter and Paul, and their dogs Nero and Brutus. But no one uses the name Judas—not even for a dog.

The significance of a name was particularly true in Bible times. In both Old and New Testaments, names were used to reflect personal experience or express or influence character:

Jacob (Gen. 25:26). Jacob (which means "supplanter") was so named because, though the second of twin brothers, he would overtake his brother, Esau, in position and significance. This was foreshadowed during his birth, and became reality as Jacob stole both the blessing and the birthright from his firstborn brother.

Naomi (Ruth 1:20). The name Naomi means "delightful one." Upon her return from the land of Moab, however, she changed her name to Mara, meaning "bitter." Why? Because in Moab she had suffered the bitter loss of a husband, two sons, and a daughter-in-law.

Samuel (1 Sam. 1:20). In the opening chapter of 1 Samuel, Hannah, in extreme anguish of heart, prayed intensely for God to give a life to her barren womb and bless her with a son. She promised to commit that son to the work of God among His people Israel. God graciously granted her request and gave her a son, who would be the final judge of Israel. He would also anoint Israel's first two kings, Saul and David. The name she gave to that son was Samuel, which means "heard of God," because God had heard and granted her request.

Barnabas (Acts 4:36). In the New Testament, we find a man named Joseph, who was so active in caring for people and encouraging others that he received a new name—a nickname. That name was Barnabas, which means "son of consolation" or "son of encouragement."

Names are important to the people of the Bible. Nowhere is this more significant than in the one who, according to the New Testament, has a name that means "Savior." In Matthew 1:21, we read words attributed to an angelic messenger speaking to Joseph:

> *She will bring forth a Son, and you shall call His name Jesus, for He will save His people from their sins.*

The name Jesus means "Jehovah our Savior." It is the New Testament equivalent of the Hebrew name Joshua, Yeshua, or Hoshea. While others wore these names in honor of God, Jesus bore His name as an expression of the Savior-God that the New Testament says He was.

Whether or not we have accepted the claims of the New Testament regarding Christ, it's important for us to see that the Scriptures honor the name Jesus for several reasons. According to them:

- *It is the name by which we must be saved.* "Nor is there salvation in any other, for there is no other name under heaven given among men by which we must be saved" (Acts 4:12).
- *It is the name that is to set the tone for everything a Christian does.* "Whatever you do in word or deed, do all in the name of the Lord Jesus, giving thanks to God the Father through Him" (Col. 3:17).
- *It is the name at which, one day in the future, every knee shall bow.* "That at the name of Jesus every knee should bow, of those in heaven, and of

those on earth, and of those under the earth, and that every tongue should confess that Jesus Christ is Lord, to the glory of God the Father" (Phil. 2:10-11).

It is just as clear, however, that from the time of Jesus' birth until now, many have missed or dismissed the significance of His name. In the days of His childhood, His neighbors knew Him as the son of Joseph the carpenter. In our generation, many of our neighbors know Jesus only as an expression of anger, alarm, or profanity. Many more have only a casual understanding of the scores of additional names given to Him in the Bible. For that reason, in the following pages we will look at four significant names that are used in anticipation of a coming Messiah more than 600 years before the birth of Jesus.

As we consider these names, keep in mind that while others use aliases to hide their true identity, the Scriptures use many names for Christ to help us get to know Him. By discovering that He is a person of many names, we will be led deeper into an understanding of who He is and why He deserves our trust.

The Predicted Names Of Messiah

No Old Testament prophet had more to say about the promised Messiah of Israel than the prophet Isaiah. In a period spanning at least 64 years, Isaiah (whose name means "the salvation of Jehovah") was God's spokesman to Israel during the reigns of four kings—Uzziah (or Azariah), Jotham, Ahaz, and Hezekiah.

Isaiah predicted a coming messianic age marked by world peace. He foresaw a world government in the last days that would turn the eyes of the international community on Jerusalem (Isa. 2:1-4). He also described the coming of a Servant-Ruler who would bring a mysterious blend of power and suffering (Isa. 53; 61:1-3). But the character of this coming Servant is most clearly stated in Isaiah 9:6, where the prophet declared:

> *Unto us a Child is born, unto us a Son is given; and the government will be upon His shoulder. And His name will be called Wonderful Counselor, Mighty God, Everlasting Father, Prince of Peace.*

Here, Isaiah says several things that remained a mystery until the coming of Christ. While it was clear that he was predicting a coming world leader and the inevitability of a messianic age, what could not have been seen until after Jesus' life, death, and resurrection is that Isaiah was actually predicting the arrival of the Son of God. All of this we can now see packed tightly and profoundly into a series of names Isaiah used for the coming Servant of God.

Before we look more closely at these names, let's review the scope of this amazing prophecy. Let's share the wonder of a passage that could be understood clearly only after the prophecy's partial fulfillment in the first coming of Christ.

The Birth Of Messiah. *"Unto us a Child is born, unto us a Son is given . . . and His name will be called . . . Mighty God, Everlasting Father, Prince of Peace."* Because of such prophecies, generations of Jewish women dreamed of being the mother who would give birth to the promised and long-awaited Messiah.

Ever since the Bethlehem arrival of Jesus, it has been clear that this prophecy anticipated far more than the birth of an eventual world leader. We can now see in the phrase "unto us a Son is given" the entrance of God's own Son into the human race that He had created.

The Kingdom Of Messiah. "*. . . and the government will be upon His shoulder . . . .*" These are words filled with both prophetic and practical significance. Prophetically, Isaiah saw the day when a son of Israel would bear upon his shoulder the weight of world leadership. In chapter 2, Isaiah predicted that in the last days the house of the Lord would be established in Jerusalem. He said the Lord Himself would "judge between the nations, and rebuke many people; they shall beat their swords into plowshares, and their spears into pruning hooks; nation shall not lift up sword against nation, neither shall they learn war anymore" (Isa. 2:4). Revelation, the last book of the New Testament, says that on that day an angel of God will declare, "The kingdoms of this world have become the kingdoms of our Lord and of His Christ [or Messiah], and He shall reign forever and ever!" (Rev. 11:15).

> The shoulders that will bear the government of the world are large enough to bear the weight of all of the problems of all of His people.

Those who have bowed their knee to this coming

Messiah and Lord can find present encouragement in that future day. While we regard as mythology the image of Atlas bearing on his shoulder the globe of the world, we can see in God's Messiah a real Lord who can carry the combined weight of all human problems. Inexpressible comfort can be found as we discover that the "shoulders" which will someday carry the government of the world are large enough to bear any personal weight or burden that we bring to Him now.

The Character Of Messiah. "*. . . and His name will be called . . . .*" Remember, Hebrew names are significant. In this final portion of the verse, the prophet used a marvelously descriptive set of names to unfold to us the very essence of the person of the Messiah. In order to give us a full understanding of the coming Redeemer, Isaiah used four compound names, each giving a different window through which to view the Son of God who was to become the Son of man for us. These four names shape our understanding of who God's Messiah is. They can help us develop a personal relationship with Him, and show us in moments of fear where to find Him.

Let's take these names one at a time. The first of them is "Wonderful Counselor."

A Guiding Name:
"WONDERFUL COUNSELOR"

"Unto us a Child is born, unto us a Son is given . . . .
And His name will be called Wonderful Counselor."

What is the meaning of the name "Wonderful Counselor"? This name literally translates, "a wonder of a counselor." But what does it mean? Let's look at it in two parts.

"Wonderful." The first is the word *Wonderful.* The Hebrew word *pala* indicates "something uncommon or out of the ordinary." It reflects "a phenomenon lying outside the realm of human explanation; that which is separated from the normal course of events; something that cannot be explained."

The same Hebrew word is used in Psalm 139:6 in just this way: "Such knowledge is too wonderful for me; it is high, I cannot attain it." It is something miraculous! The problem is that we have a low view of the miraculous, and therefore a limited sense of wonder.

> Wonder is found not merely in what is difficult to explain, but in that which cannot be captured by human reason.

Think of some of the ways we routinely use the word *miracle.* In 1980, when the US Hockey Team won gold in the Olympics, Al Michaels' now-famous cry was, "Do you believe in miracles? Yes!" In a once-popular television ad, a monk is able to get productive work out of his photocopier, and all present exclaim, "It's a miracle." A college student comes out of a classroom holding her exam paper, which bears the grade "A+" and says to her friend, "This is a miracle! I didn't think I was anywhere near ready for that test."

In reality, however, those things are not miracles. They can all be explained—though some may take a little more effort to explain than others.

Do we have a sense of wonder that goes beyond all human, rational explanation? Or have the successes of human science and technology robbed us of our ability to worship a God of miracles? Do we honestly believe that the greatest "miracles" are not come-from-behind victories by our favorite sports team, or the latest in technological wizardry, or the wonder drug that calmed our hay fever? All of those can be explained.

A real wonder is something beyond human explanation. And the prophet Isaiah declared that the coming Child and Son would be a wonder. This not only describes what He does, it describes who He is. Do you see Him that way? He, Himself, is the wonder!

"Counselor." The second part of this compound description of the coming Messiah is *Counselor.* In its historical Hebrew usage, the word is used to picture a king giving counsel to his people. To that end, Micah declared the dilemma of the captives in Babylon this way, "Now why do you cry aloud? Is there no king in your midst? Has your counselor perished?" (4:9).

Long before the Child was ever born, long before the Son was given, Isaiah foretold that God was planning to send a Counselor for the brokenhearted people of the world. And long after Jesus' entrance into the world we can see that He personified the kind of counsel that will go out from Jerusalem in the last days.

- "He will teach us His ways, and we shall walk in His paths. For out of Zion shall go forth the law, and the word of the Lord from Jerusalem" (Isa. 2:3).
- ". . . the Spirit of wisdom and understanding" (Isa. 11:2).
- ". . . the Lord of hosts, who is wonderful in counsel and excellent in guidance" (Isa. 28:29).

What is the evidence that Jesus Christ is the Wonderful Counselor? For us who live on this side of the life, death, and resurrection of Christ, these statements are not just theory. We can see them fleshed out in a Person. We now can read, and reflect, and appeal for help from the One "who became for us wisdom from God" (1 Cor. 1:30). From our point in history we can see that Jesus is the very wisdom of God.

We now can see the principle of wisdom fleshed out in a Person of unlimited understanding.

When you take all that we know about Christ, it adds up to a marvelous truth—He is the God who is, and who is called, a "Wonder of a Counselor."

His Wonder. If a wonder is anything that excites amazement, then it describes everything about the One who came in fulfillment of Isaiah's prophecy. In 1 Timothy 3:16, Paul expressed the wonder of the Lord who clothed Himself in human flesh:

Without controversy great is the mystery of godliness: God was manifested in the flesh, justified in the

*Spirit, seen by angels, preached among the Gentiles,
believed on in the world, received up in glory.*

The wonder of this brief statement disturbs philosophers, delights beggars, and comforts the brokenhearted. It speaks of the Hero of heaven who gathers little children to Himself. He is the Son of God who offers to bring people of all nations to His Father, and who invites all who trust Him to be part of His family forever.

What He did in His work of redemption for us is beyond comprehension. Try to imagine what it will mean to enjoy for all eternity a wondering, worshiping, loving relationship with the Creator God, the Son of heaven who became sin for us (2 Cor. 5:20-21). Think about Him: God the Son, deity in every way, yet willing to bear our sins in His body on the tree. Everything about Him should stir our hearts in wonder-filled submission!

His Counsel. Even as a child of 12, Jesus astounded Jewish rabbis with His wisdom (Lk. 2:46-47). Luke recorded that "the Child grew and became strong in spirit, filled with wisdom; and the grace of God was upon Him" (2:40). In His public life, people were amazed at the truthfulness of His counsel. "When He had come to His own country, He taught them in their synagogue, so that they were astonished and said, 'Where did this Man get this wisdom and these mighty works?'" (Mt. 13:54). Later, the apostle Paul wrote that in Him "are hidden all the treasures of wisdom and knowledge" (Col. 2:3).

It's appropriate, then, to ask ourselves whether we

are as astonished at the wonder of a counselor as Isaiah was. Are we captivated by His charm, insight, and practical genius? Where else can we go to learn how to love, how to cry, how to live, and how to die? Where else can we be so assured of the acceptance and forgiveness and comfort of God? Where else can we look into a face that is the face of our Creator, Savior, and Counselor?

What is the importance of the name "Wonderful Counselor" to believers today? How does this "Wonder of a Counselor" give us help? How does He impart His wisdom, and how should we seek it? It would be a serious error to think that we can now come to Him the way a person comes to a fortune teller or a spiritual medium.

Because the Wonderful Counselor whom Isaiah predicted is also our Creator and Savior, and because He is the fulfillment of all that both Old and New Testaments teach, His counsel is found wherever we can find the words and provisions of God.

The Old Testament is His story. The New Testament Gospels are the record of His conversations with the people of His day. The letters of the rest of the New Testament represent the practical application of His teaching to life.

We find His counsel in the Sermon on the Mount, and in His conversations with Peter, James, and John. We find His teaching and wisdom in the letters of the apostle Paul. We find His insight in the letters to the seven churches of Revelation.

Our Wonderful Counselor urges us to let Him

bring us to the Father. He offers Himself as the sacrifice for our sin and the basis of our acceptance with God. He offers to be for us everything we need for this life and the next. He was not just telling us what we want to hear when He reassuringly said:

> Do not worry, saying, "What shall we eat?" or "What shall we drink?" or "What shall we wear?" For after all these things the Gentiles seek. For your heavenly Father knows that you need all these things. But seek first the kingdom of God and His righteousness, and all these things shall be added to you. Therefore do not worry about tomorrow, for tomorrow will worry about its own things. Sufficient for the day is its own trouble (Mt. 6:31-34).

How then does our Wonderful Counselor help us with our problems and lead us to a place of security, satisfaction, and enjoyment? He does so through His Word and prayer (Ps. 119:24; Jas. 1:5). He does so by reminding us that there is safety in a multitude of good counselors (Prov. 11:14). But most of all He does so with the assurance that because of who He is He can help us in ways that go far beyond our ability to understand (Ps. 32:8).

Our Wonderful Counselor's ability to help us goes far beyond the limited help that we are able to offer one another.

I was reminded of our own limitations to help one another while on a brief stopover in London on a return trip from Israel. While standing on a corner of Oxford Street, a man came to me and asked me for directions to a certain place in London (where I had now been for a total of about 18 hours). No matter how concerned I was for this man, or how sincerely I wanted him to reach his destination, the problem was that he was asking the wrong person for directions. I simply was not equipped to give him the guidance he needed (and told him so).

Christ is able to give us the needed direction for life. How thankful we should be that Isaiah spoke of a Wonderful Counselor, who is also rightly named the "Mighty God."

A Powerful Name:
"MIGHTY GOD"

"Unto us a Child is born, unto us a Son is given . . . . And His name will be called . . . Mighty God."

What is the meaning of the name "Mighty God"? The name "Mighty God" is an Old Testament title here applied to the coming Messiah. It is the compound Hebrew *El Gibbor*, and both parts of the name need to be understood.

"God." The first part of the title is *El*, which is used in the Old Testament to refer to the one true God (though on occasion it is used of mighty heroes, or even false gods). It is the singular form of the word *Elohim*.

Even though Jesus Himself pointed out that the title is sometimes used of mighty sons of men (Jn. 10:34), the title is so often used of God, and only God, that the prophet Hosea used *El* to set God in contrast to man in Hosea 11:9. Isaiah himself used *El* in the same way when he declared, "Now the Egyptians are men, and not God [lit. *El*]; and their horses are flesh, and not spirit. When the Lord stretches out His hand, both he who helps will fall, and he who is helped will fall down; they all will perish together" (Isa. 31:3).

> **The Messiah would not only have the power of God, He would *be* the God of power!**

That Isaiah 9:6 was predicting One who would be far more than a man is indicated not only by the third name "Everlasting Father" and by other prophetic references such as Isaiah 2:1-4, but by the New Testament record of Christ. The Christ who walked on water, died voluntarily for our sin, and then rose bodily from the dead is the One who also said, "Before Abraham was, I am" (Jn. 8:58). He is the One of whom John wrote:

> *In the beginning was the Word, and the Word was with God, and the Word was God. He was in the beginning with God. All things were made through Him, and without Him nothing was made that was made (Jn. 1:1-3).*

"Mighty." The other part of the name is *Gibbor*, which means "strength, power, hero." What a statement! In a world where heroes are determined by their athletic prowess or financial power, we are told that the only One truly worthy to be adored is the One whose might is unparalleled! Isaiah 10:21 describes Him as the refuge of the remnant, and Deuteronomy 10:17 declares that He is the "great God, mighty and awesome."

The focus of Isaiah's prophecy is *El Gibbor*, the Mighty God who is our true Hero. What this prophet in the seventh century BC anticipated, the New Testament confirms. Because the Messiah would be God, He would have God's power. But to Isaiah, the amazing thing was that the Messiah would not only have the power of God, He would be the God of power!

In other parts of his prophecy, Isaiah gave more details of what this mighty power would look like. For instance, in a messianic section of his prophecy, Isaiah declared:

> *The Spirit of the Lord God is upon Me, because the Lord has anointed Me to preach good tidings to the poor; He has sent Me to heal the brokenhearted, to proclaim liberty to the captives, and the opening of the prison to those who are bound; to proclaim the acceptable year of the Lord, and the day of vengeance of our God; to comfort all who mourn, to console those who mourn in Zion, to give them beauty for ashes, the oil of joy for mourning, the garment of praise for the spirit of heaviness; that they may be called trees of righteousness, the planting of the Lord, that He may be glorified (61:1-3).*

What is the evidence that Jesus Christ is the "Mighty God"? Jesus used Isaiah 61:1-3 to make His claim as the Messiah (Lk. 4:16-21). But because He only partially fulfilled this prophecy in His first coming, He was only partially recognized. By His resurrection, perfect life, sacrificial death, and many mighty signs He showed we could trust Him to return one day to rule the world. Most of His own people rejected Him. John wrote, "He came to His own, and His own did not receive Him" (Jn. 1:11).

In many cases, however, He was recognized as the long-awaited Messiah. Nicodemus, a rabbi of Israel, recognized Him (cp. Jn. 3 with Jn. 19). The disciples recognized Him (cp. Mt. 8:27 with 16:16). Mary Magdalene recognized Him, and her life was transformed (Lk. 8:2). Others' lives were changed as well, even the life of the church's most feared persecutor, Saul of Tarsus (Acts 9).

These and thousands of other first-century Jews believed—and for good reason. Jesus Christ proved Himself to be *El Gibbor* as He displayed His life-changing might and power.

For those who see their need of a Savior, the evidence of Christ's mighty power is overwhelming. For those who sense their own weakness and inability to live up to God's standard, the apostle John wrote, "As many as received Him, to them He gave the right to become children of God, to those who believe in His name" (Jn. 1:12).

What the New Testament provides is an opportunity to see the fullness of the "Mighty God" Isaiah was predicting. Before we go on, let's make sure we understand what a Mighty God our Savior and Champion is to those who trust Him.

Jesus as the Mighty God before His birth. The clear statement of the Word of God is that Christ displayed His might in the creation of the world before He physically entered the world. John 1:3 says,

"All things were made through Him, and without Him nothing was made that was made." Colossians 1:16 agrees: "For by Him all things were created that are in heaven and that are on earth, visible and invisible, whether thrones or dominions or principalities or powers. All things were created through Him and for Him."

Christ displayed His might in the very act of creation itself, and He did so in a way that distinguished Him from mere men. Man has the ability to make things, but he requires some basic raw materials. Christ, however, showed His might in the ability to create—to make something out of nothing! While ingenuity, genius, and creativity are all commendable and necessary in inventing and making new things, it takes divine might to create. Christ demonstrated that power in the most profound way.

Jesus as the Mighty God during His earthly life. Look at the way Jesus showed His right to be recognized as the Mighty God that Isaiah predicted. He demonstrated power over nature (Lk. 5:1-11), power over disease (Mt. 9:18-26), power over demons (Lk. 8:26-39), power over sin (Mk. 2:3-12), and power over death (1 Cor. 15:1-19). Throughout the course of His public life, Christ revealed His divine might in ways that not only were undeniable (Acts 2:22), but were also intentional validations of His claim of deity (Jn. 20:30-31). When we see the otherwise inexplicable demonstrations of the might and power of God in the unparalleled life of Christ, it becomes clear why Paul would call Jesus "the Son of God with power"

(Rom. 1:4) and "Christ the power of God and the wisdom of God" (1 Cor. 1:24).

What is the importance of the name "Mighty God" to believers today? In the midst of evidence that shows Christ to be the Mighty God, it is important to remember that this is more than just theological data. It is divinely inspired evidence that urges us to see and respond to Christ as He is—our "Mighty God."

He is the source of our power. In Acts 1:8, Jesus promised to send the power of the Holy Spirit to enable us to be His representatives in all the world. Inherent to this provision of the Spirit is the fact that He wants us to live distinguishable lives and to display an honesty of heart in an impure world as evidence of His presence in us.

He is the strength of our lives. In Philippians 4:13, Paul wrote, "I can do all things through Christ who strengthens me." What a great promise! He will strengthen us for all the circumstances and inevitabilities of life. This doesn't mean that we will never know pain or hardship, but that we, by His might, can endure hardness as good soldiers of Jesus Christ. How can we do that? Only as we do it in His power, not in our own.

He secures our eternity. The apostle Peter wrote that we are "kept by the power of God" (1 Pet. 1:5). Nothing can overcome the divine power that keeps us in Christ. What a great assurance it is to know that we are not secure because of our own strength to hold on to Him, but because of His power by which He holds on to us.

In view of the predictive evidence of Isaiah and the historic record of the Gospels, how can we see our Lord Jesus Christ as anything less than the Mighty God, *El Gibbor*? In 1885, J. B. Figgis described in his book *Emmanuel* the surprising yet ingenious way in which the Mighty God showed Himself by miracles, as well as by His disarming display of approachable meekness:

> Christ's inimitable meekness and patience never once forsook Him in a vexatious, ungrateful, cruel sphere. He never stepped out of the humble sphere in which He was brought up; He does not seem to have ever possessed for Himself so much as the smallest coin, and when He died had no means for providing for His mother, and could only commend her to one of His disciples. Yet, His life was infinitely superior to all others. If Jesus were no more than a man or a hero, why are there not more men like Him? What God did for one man, God would certainly do for others. It is unaccountable that it has never been done. The incarnation, when Jesus came as "the Mighty God," alone helps us to the solution of such an enigma.

A Timeless Name:
"EVERLASTING FATHER"

*"Unto us a Child is born, unto us a Son is given . . . .
And His name will be called . . . Everlasting Father."*

What is the meaning of the name "Everlasting Father"? This name offers honor that goes far beyond recognition given to the Jewish national father Abraham. For centuries it was a name, like "Mighty God," that was shrouded in mystery. What mortal could bear such a name?

The symbolic use of the word *father* was an ancient Hebraism for "possessor of." Notice that in Isaiah 9:6 the Messiah is described as both a Son ("unto us a Son is given") and a Father ("His name will be called . . . Everlasting Father"). He became a child in time (through the incarnation), but He is the Father (and possessor) of eternity. This means several basic things:

He inhabits and possesses eternity. "For thus says the High and Lofty One who inhabits eternity, whose name is Holy: 'I dwell in the high and holy place, with him who has a contrite and humble spirit, to revive the spirit of the humble, and to revive the heart of the contrite ones'" (Isa. 57:15).

His name is eternal. "His name shall endure forever; His name shall continue as long as the sun. And men shall be blessed in Him; all nations shall call Him blessed" (Ps. 72:17).

He is the eternal provider. "He said to me, 'It is done! I am the Alpha and the Omega, the Beginning and the End. I will give of the fountain of the water of life freely to him who thirsts. He who overcomes shall inherit all things, and I will be his God and he shall be My son'" (Rev. 21:6-7).

He is eternal in all that He is and all that He does! This implies several crucial truths claimed for God's Messiah in both Old and New Testaments:

He is preexistent. "Before the mountains were brought forth, or ever You had formed the earth and the world, even from everlasting to everlasting, You are God" (Ps. 90:2).

He is self-existent. In Exodus 3 we find the name "I Am." This name describes and defines the God who is. He is totally independent of His creation, and totally independent of time. He is the God who is Alpha and Omega, the God of the eternal present tense. As self-existent, He is wholly and completely self-dependent. Frederick Faber wrote, "No age can keep its outward years on Thee, dear God! Thou art, Thyself, Thine own eternity."

What is the evidence that Jesus Christ is the "Everlasting Father"? In the events recorded in John 8:12-58, a fascinating dialog occurs. The exchange is between Jesus and His religious antagonists, the Pharisees. Jesus called God His Father. The Pharisees called Abraham their father. Jesus said that if Abraham were their father they would do the works of Abraham. They responded that at least they were not born of fornication (implying that Mary had been sexually active before marriage), and then matched Jesus' claim that all have one Father—God. To this Jesus replied:

If God were your Father, you would love Me, for I proceeded forth and came from God; nor have I come of Myself, but He sent Me. Why do you not understand My speech? Because you are not able to listen to My word. You are of your father the devil, and the desires of your father you want to do (Jn. 8:42-44).

The Pharisees were making their claim to Abraham and to the God of Abraham, but Jesus wasn't backing down. More important, He clarified that their link to Abraham was only physical. Spiritually they were of their father the devil.

Then Jesus made the most amazing statement of all. He said, "Before Abraham was, I AM" (Jn. 8:58). To His countrymen, He had finally gone too far. They recognized that by such a claim He was making Himself equal with God. (In Exodus 3:14, Moses met the God who identified Himself as the "I AM WHO I AM.") As on several other occasions, Jesus so infuriated the Pharisees that they picked up stones with the intent to kill Him.

> When Jesus said, "Before Abraham was, I AM," He linked Himself to the "Everlasting Father" Isaiah foresaw.

In retrospect, we can see more than the Pharisees' rage. We can also see One who by His miraculous life, death, and resurrection has shown His right to the name Isaiah's prophecy had given to the Messiah 600 years before Jesus' birth.

The truth of the eternality of the Messiah is something that has come under continuous attack for centuries. But the inescapable fact is that all groups who reject the eternality of Christ also reject His deity. The two are inseparable! If Jesus is not eternal, He is not God—and vice versa. Yet Isaiah said that when Messiah came, He would be the physical embodiment of the Everlasting Father.

The ability of Christ to be a timeless source of fatherly protection and provision is claimed in a number of ways in the New Testament.

- His character is described as eternally consistent and immutable (unchanging). Hebrews 13:8 says, "Jesus Christ is the same yesterday, today, and forever."
- His New Testament title Alpha and Omega (Rev. 1:8) uses the first (alpha) and last (omega) letter of the Greek alphabet to symbolize that Christ is before everything and will surpass everything.
- He declared that His divine judgment will be an eternal one (Mt. 18:8).
- John the Baptist, whose birth preceded Jesus, still recognized the eternality of Christ when he said, "This is He of whom I said, 'After me comes a Man who is preferred before me, for He was before me'" (Jn. 1:30). He is the eternal One!

What is the importance of the name "Everlasting Father" to believers today? The self-existence of God's Messiah means that He will not leave us, as all earthly fathers eventually do. This, among many other facts, makes the incarnation an amazing thing. The Eternal God took upon Himself the limitations of a human body so that He could bring us into an everlasting relationship with Himself.

The New Testament reminds us that it is not proper for the children of God to act as if we do not have all that we need. Even though this world is marked by unfairness, inequality, and suffering, those of us who believe in God's Messiah are in the hands of an Eternal Father and Provider.

Let your conduct be without covetousness; be content with such things as you have. For He Himself has said, "I will never leave you nor forsake you" (Heb. 13:5).

A. W. Tozer wrote, "We poor human creatures are constantly being frustrated by the limitations imposed on us. The days of the years of our lives are short! Life is a short and fevered rehearsal for a concert we cannot stay to give. Just when we appear to have gained some proficiency, we are forced to lay our instruments down" (*The Knowledge Of The Holy*, p.52). This is true, and it demands that we turn from our limitations to an uninhibited dependence on the Father of Eternity who has no limitations!

This is the Father who will never leave us:

- He provides the strength of "everlasting arms" (Dt. 33:27).
- He ministers with an "everlasting consolation" (2 Th. 2:16).
- He performs His work with "everlasting power" (1 Tim. 6:16).
- He rules over an "everlasting kingdom" (2 Pet. 2:11).
- He maintains an eternal presence (Mt. 28:20).
- He gives us life that is eternal (Jn. 14:19).

- He graciously provides for those who realize that the values that will never end are what really count (Mt. 6:33).

Eternal values are not easy to think about. But we cannot afford to ignore them! It is of everlasting profit for us to ponder the timeless vastness of our God. If He were only God for the length of our lifetime here on earth, He would still deserve our reverence and trust. But as the God of eternity, He is worthy of our fullest, unending devotion and most careful attention.

Someone has said that the most important thing about us is what we believe about God. In that light, consider again the words of A. W. Tozer:

> It is not a cheerful thought that millions of us who live in the land of Bibles, who belong to churches and labor to promote the Christian religion, may yet pass our whole life on this earth without once having thought or tried to think seriously about the being of God. Few of us have let our hearts gaze in wonder at the I AM, the self-existent Self, back of which no creature can think. Such thoughts are too painful for us. We prefer to think where it will do more good—about how to make a better mousetrap, for instance, or how to make two blades of grass grow where one grew before. And for this we are now paying a too heavy price in the secularization of our religion, and the decay of our inner lives (*The Knowledge Of The Holy*, p.34).

May we take time to think about Christ, the timeless One who invaded time to rescue us from sin and self, the Father of Eternity who has given eternal life to make it possible for us to have eternal peace with God and with one another.

A Comforting Name:
"PRINCE OF PEACE"

*"Unto us a Child is born, unto us a Son is given . . . .
And His name will be called . . . Prince of Peace."*

What is the meaning of the name "Prince of Peace"?
The name "Prince of Peace" is the Hebrew *Shar Shalom*,
which means "the one who removes all peace-disturbing
factors and secures the peace." This automatically sets
Him apart from most human rulers whose reigns often
depend on bloody conquest. His rule rests on a bloody
sacrifice! What a contrast to such biblical kings as
Nebuchadnezzar, and even David, whose rule was
established on might, but not necessarily on right.

The name "Peaceful Prince" helps to explain why
Jesus disappointed His countrymen when He came!
They did not want a peaceful prince. They wanted a
monarch who would annihilate their foes and establish again the glories the kingdom of Israel knew in
the golden days of Solomon. They wanted Rome
taken away and all their other oppressors with them.

Peace or a sword? Jesus didn't lift a finger against
Rome. He didn't make one international peace treaty.
How can He then be considered the Prince of Peace?
Notice two very different statements from the New
Testament: Luke 2:14 states, "Glory to God in the
highest, and on earth peace, goodwill toward men!"
But in Matthew 10:34, Jesus said, "Do not think that
I came to bring peace on earth. I did not come to
bring peace but a sword."

How can these two statements be reconciled? Can we blame Jesus' countrymen for rejecting the Prince of Peace if our own world is still engulfed in conflict as we move into the third millennium?

The two phases of peace. The answer of the New Testament must be considered. It claims that the first phase of His coming was to establish a basis for peace with God and to offer it to individuals of all nations. The New Testament also claims that He will come a second time to bring peace to the earth.

If the New Testament can be trusted, Jesus will bring peace in two phases.

According to the apostle Paul, the first phase of Messiah's coming produced a peace unknown to man since the fall of Adam into sin. It is rooted in the saving mission carried out by Christ on our behalf. Paul wrote:

> *God was in Christ reconciling the world to Himself, not imputing their trespasses to them, and has committed to us the word of reconciliation (2 Cor. 5:19).*

This means that the peace Jesus brought is more than a negotiated ceasefire between ourselves and God. It is a peace that changes us from enemies into the children of God.

What is the evidence that Jesus Christ is the "Prince of Peace"? This is seen in a variety of ways in the New Testament Scriptures:

His power. So significant was the power of the Son of God that He was able to bring calm to the natural storms on the turbulent Sea of Galilee. "He arose and rebuked the wind, and said to the sea, 'Peace, be still!' And the wind ceased and there was a great calm" (Mk. 4:39).

His cross. So effective is His work on the cross that it is able to make peace between God and man. "It pleased the Father . . . by Him to reconcile all things to Himself, by Him, whether things on earth or things in heaven, having made peace through the blood of His cross. And you, who once were alienated and enemies in your mind by wicked works, yet now He has reconciled" (Col. 1:19-21).

His gospel. The good news of salvation in Christ is acknowledged as the root of peace in the hearts of the redeemed. "The word which God sent to the children of Israel, preaching peace through Jesus Christ— He is Lord of all" (Acts 10:36).

His body. Though Judaism separated Jews and Gentiles, Christ has not only reconciled God and man, He has reconciled Jew and Gentile so that we are now one body in Christ. "He Himself is our peace, who has made both one, and has broken down the middle wall of separation" (Eph. 2:14).

What is the importance of the name "Prince of Peace" to the believer today? Those who trust Christ as their Mediator and Savior are given by God an assurance that flows out of a right relationship with Him. Once we are in Christ, the Prince of Peace shows us that He can bring peace wherever He rules. He can bring:

Peace in life's trials. "Peace I leave with you, My peace I give to you; not as the world gives do I give to you. Let not your heart be troubled, neither let it be afraid" (Jn. 14:27).

Peace in life's maturing process. "Now may the God of peace Himself sanctify you completely; and may your whole spirit, soul, and body be preserved blameless at the coming of our Lord Jesus Christ" (1 Th. 5:23).

Peace in life's victories. "The God of peace will crush Satan under your feet shortly" (Rom. 16:20).

Peace in life's relationships. ". . . endeavoring to keep the unity of the Spirit in the bond of peace" (Eph. 4:3).

Peace in life's witness. "The fruit of the Spirit is love, joy, peace, longsuffering, kindness, goodness, faithfulness, gentleness, self-control" (Gal. 5:22-23).

What a treasure is ours in Isaiah's predicted Messiah. He is our Wonderful Counselor, Mighty God, Everlasting Father, and Prince of Peace. May we give Him worship, as we ponder the great God that He is!

What Do You Call Him?

Jesus asked His disciples two questions: "Who do men say that I am?" and "Who do you say that I am?" (Mk. 8:27,29). The first question is significant because it allows us to get a read on the minds of the people around us. The second question, however, is eternal because it is only by acknowledging Jesus Christ and responding to His gift of forgiveness by faith that a person can live forever.

Isaiah made it very clear that when the promised Messiah would come, He would fulfill the matchless titles he had prophesied: "Wonderful Counselor," "Mighty God," "Everlasting Father," and "Prince of Peace." Jesus Christ came into the world and proved beyond a doubt that He was the Messiah by fulfilling all those requirements. He was God in human flesh, come to display deity and redeem humanity. And on the strength of His ability to fulfill all these things, He made this claim: "No one comes to the Father except through Me" (Jn. 14:6).

This is the claim of the Bible, and the heartbeat of the Christian faith: Jesus Christ is God and He came into the world to save sinners. What is your response to that claim and to the evidence that He is the only deliverer for sin-laden, lost people who are the object of God's love? Will you receive His gift of forgiveness and be saved?

If you are already saved, having been rescued from your sin and its just punishment, will you live under His perfect will and wisdom so that He may guide you into a life that pleases Him? May it ever be so, for He brings peace wherever He reigns!

2

Who Is This Man Who Says He's God?

No one would argue the identity of people like Lincoln, Michelangelo, or Aristotle. They wear history-book labels that are indisputable. But the man called Jesus is different. If you were to run a man-on-the-street survey about Him, you would likely get as many different responses as you would get odd looks. Jesus isn't known for the things that usually make people famous. He wasn't into politics, business, or publishing. His expertise was in what we normally call religion—He knew a lot about God. In fact, He claimed to be God. But who is He? This booklet by Dave Branon has been written to help you discover who the Bible says Jesus is.

Martin R. De Haan II

Who Doesn't Believe
That Jesus Is God?

Many people peer back through the darkened pages of history and see a rather obscure picture of Jesus. They have heard of His 2,000-year-old claim that He was God, but they don't quite believe it. They find it hard to accept the idea that a small-town Jewish carpenter could have been the creator of the world. They prefer to believe other, less sensational theories about Him. Here are some of those beliefs.

Jesus is a man who achieved great things. Among the groups who hold to this view is the Church Of Jesus Christ Of Latter Day Saints—the Mormons. They teach that Jesus was a preexistent spirit—but they believe that about everyone. They say that Jesus' distinctiveness is not that He was God, but that He was God's firstborn spirit-child. "His humanity is to be recognized as real and ordinary—whatever happened to Him may happen to any of us" (Elder B. H. Roberts citing Sir Oliver Lodge in *Joseph Smith, King Follett Discourse,* p.11 note).

Jesus is a created being who was given the status of second-in-command. According to the Jehovah's Witnesses, Jesus is "a god, but not the Almighty God, who is Jehovah" (*Let God Be True,* p.33). Instead, they say that Jesus is "a created individual" who "is the second greatest personage of the universe" (*Make Sure Of All Things,* p.207).

Jesus is a man no better than we are. "It is plain that Jesus is not God Himself" (*Divine Principle,* p.255). These words of Sun Myung Moon clearly spell out the view of his Unification Church. Its teaching is that Jesus' value is no greater than that of any other man. Those who follow Moon's theology say that Jesus' work was a failure.

Jesus' existence began at His conception. One group that teaches this idea is The Way International. In their reinterpretation of biblical instruction, they hold that "Jesus Christ's existence began when he was conceived by God's creating the soul-life of Jesus in Mary" (Victor Wierwille, *The Word's Way*, Vol. 3, pp.26-27).

Jesus is a prophet and messenger of God. According to the tenets of Islam, "Jesus . . . was only a messenger of Allah" (Surah 4:171 from the *Koran*). They also say He was a sinless prophet who never achieved the greatness of the prophet Muhammad.

Jesus is less than most people think He is. Those who embrace atheism have a low view of Jesus. Some cannot find it in themselves to place Jesus on as high a plane as such past notables as Buddha or Socrates. Bertrand Russell, a famous apologist of the atheistic viewpoint, said, "I cannot myself feel that either in the matter of wisdom or in the matter of virtue Christ stands quite as high as some other people known to history" (*Why I Am Not A Christian*, p.19).

Jesus is a great moral teacher. Some people don't reject all of Jesus' work on earth, though they do reject His claims to deity. William Channing of the Unitarian church said, "Christ was sent to earth as a great moral teacher rather than as a mediator."

Jesus is a mystic medium. New Age thinkers consider Jesus to be a guide to self-actualization. In this regard, Jesus would be seen as a channel—one of many ancients who give New Age adherents a "glimpse" at the past. Through previous incarnations, they contend, He attained a level of purity that is achievable by all.

Jesus is a projection of our needs. Some feel that the only reason Jesus has reached great heights of importance is that humans need someone like Him to fall back on. Carl Jung, a famous Swiss psychologist and psychiatrist, said that Jesus is "our culture hero who, regardless of His historical existence, embodies the myth of the divine man."

One thing is for sure. Somebody is wrong! These people can't all be right about Jesus. He cannot be exactly who all these people say He is. Many who think they know, don't know. If He is only a prophet or a medium, then those who insist He is God are wrong. If on the other hand He is God, then those who insist that He is only an exceptional man are wrong. Some might wish to have it both ways. In science and investigative journalism, we pursue truth passionately. Why should it be any different in this important realm?

> Some find it hard to accept that a small-town Jewish carpenter could have been the creator of the world.

Why Is This So Important?

Most people are rather free with their complimentary descriptions and names for Jesus. He has been given such noble titles as "the second greatest person of the universe," "a prophet from God," "a great moral teacher," "a holy man," "touched by God more than anyone else." Who wouldn't be thrilled to have their leader thought of in such lofty terms? What group would be dissatisfied with this kind of respect and praise for their founder?

Christians, for one. Followers of Jesus are not satisfied with those terms. To them, it is not enough that He is considered one of history's greatest figures. Christians feel that there is more to Jesus than to be thought of by millions as an exemplary human—even the greatest man who ever lived. They think the names "moral teacher" and "prophet" don't go far enough. No, Christians insist on one more designation for Jesus—one on which the whole of Christianity rests, yet one that throws a roadblock in the way of many who might otherwise consider following Him.

Jesus' followers insist not only on calling Him Messiah and Savior but Lord and God as well. But why? What is so important about this designation for Jesus? Can't we just learn from His wise sayings and admire His good life and leave it at that? Is it all that vital that we make such an issue about whether or not He is God?

Interestingly, Jesus' deity is perhaps the most important question to answer about Christianity. Why? Because Jesus said He was God. As we will see, He proclaimed His deity on many occasions while living among His fellow Israeli citizens. Without fear of the ramifications and without regard to the skepticism of His audience, Jesus left no doubt in His listeners' minds that He was claiming to be God.

So that leaves us with a dilemma. We can't possibly trust the word of someone who said he is the Almighty God, no matter what good works he did or what wisdom he expounded—unless he really is God. Otherwise this person would only merit our pity, our concern, and our sympathy. A man who would call himself God without being God would certainly not merit our worship, our admiration, and our emulation.

> What is so important about this designation for Jesus? Can't we just learn from His wise sayings and admire His good life and leave it at that?

So what's the big deal? The big deal is that if Jesus isn't God, then He can't be an example, a wise teacher, a moral leader, or even an important historical person. Providing the evidence that He is God is the biggest issue in the world. And that's what this booklet will set out to do.

We can't afford our own customized ideas of who Jesus is. We can't afford anything less than the truth. As we'll see, our eternal destiny hangs on how we answer the question, "Who is this man who says He's God?"

What Does The Bible Say About All This?

Prove it. These two words can block the path of anyone who tries to support the truth of a statement. If a concept cannot be backed up by the evidence, it is not worth the time it takes to state it. The key to finding the necessary evidence is in finding a reliable, credible source. Without a solid source, the inquirer is left with nothing but opinions.

That's where the belief that Jesus is God finds strength. The source for this idea is a book that can be trusted—the Bible. Intense archaeological research has shown the Bible to be trustworthy in historical and geographical matters. The Scriptures have been scrutinized by scholars for nearly 2,000 years and have been found reliable. They are backed up by more manuscript findings than any other ancient document. All of these external evidences give us additional confidence in this book in which God has given His divine revelation to the human race. The deity of Christ is a concept that can be trusted because it comes from a credible source.

In that light, it makes sense for us to see what the Bible says about the identity of its central figure. It makes sense for us to follow that evidence all the way to its own conclusion. It doesn't make sense, however, to trust the Bible's description of Jesus as a teacher sent from God if we are not willing to accept what Jesus said about Himself.

If the Bible is a book to be trusted, and if its message has been miraculously preserved for us across the centuries, then we can trust it to be a valuable source for finding out about the One who preserved it. Let's look at what the Bible says about the idea that Jesus is God.

The Claims Of The Old Testament

The Bible does not sneak up on its New Testament readers and spring a new message on them. No, the idea that a Messiah would visit the earth is not a surprise to anyone who is familiar with the Old Testament. There were plenty of signals from the prophets that this would happen. In fact, there are many specific facts about the  Messiah's life predicted in the Old Testament that were fulfilled by Jesus. The chart on the following page gives just a sampling.

It's clear that the Messiah's coming was an expected event on the religious calendar of pre-Christian days. But there's more. Not only did the holy writings of the Old Testament era tell of a coming Messiah, but they also told us that He would have a quality known to no other man. He would be God. Three Old Testament verses stand out as proof that Jesus—the divinely pre-announced Messiah—was to be God in the flesh. A close look at these passages will introduce us clearly to this essential truth.

Prophecy	Reference	Fulfillment
Born of a virgin	Isaiah 7:14	Matthew 1:23
Born in Bethlehem	Micah 5:2	Matthew 2:5
Found in Egypt	Numbers 24:8	Matthew 2:15
To heal many	Isaiah 53:4	Matthew 8:16
Crucified	Isaiah 53:12	Matthew 27:38
No bones broken	Psalm 34:20	John 19:33-36

Isaiah 7:14. *"Behold, the virgin shall conceive and bear a Son, and shall call His name Immanuel."* The key to seeing this verse as a prediction of Jesus' coming as God in the flesh is found in the title Immanuel. The word literally means "God with us." Surely this must have been a mystery to those who heard this prophecy. In what sense would the child bear the presence of God?

Because of the additional revelation of the New Testament (Mt. 1:21-23), we can understand what they could not. We can see a pre-indicator of God's plan to visit the earth, not merely through a spokesman and savior, but through One who would literally be "God with us." But what about the Old Testament's point of view? What other evidence can we find?

Isaiah 9:6. *"For unto us a Child is born, unto us a Son is given; and the government will be upon His shoulder. And His name will be called Wonderful Counselor, Mighty God, Everlasting Father, Prince of Peace."*

Looking back, we can once again see an amazing prophecy in perspective. All who recognize Jesus as this Messiah are told by the Old Testament prophet that He would not only be a ruler but would also be "Mighty God."

This is the same term and the same grammatical construction the prophet used in Isaiah 10:21 in saying that "the remnant of Jacob" shall return to "the Mighty God." This leaves us with only two possibilities. First, the prophet could be telling us that another "Mighty God" would be coming—giving the world two Gods. Yet that would contradict other verses such as Isaiah 45:22, which says, "Look to Me, and be saved, all you ends of the earth! For I am God, and there is no other." That refutation of a two-God system leaves us with one other conclusion. The Jehovah whom Isaiah and his people worshiped and the Son-Child who would be born and called "Mighty God" had to be the same.

Micah 5:2. *"But you, Bethlehem Ephrathah, though you are little among the thousands of Judah, yet out of you shall come forth to Me the One to be ruler in Israel, whose goings forth have been from of old, from everlasting."*

To live forever. It's an idea that intrigues us all but is impossible to achieve. While it's true that our souls will live forever, no one can claim to have been present with God before the world began. No one but Jesus, that is. Not only did Micah predict that Jesus would be born in Bethlehem, but he also revealed that this "ruler in Israel" has shared the counsels of God from eternity past. How does this prove Jesus' deity? If only God has existed from eternity past, and Jesus existed with Him, then He has to be God.

Clearly, all who recognize Jesus as Messiah recognize that something amazing happened when Jesus appeared on the scene. At the very least, He fulfilled prophecies in a miraculous way. One researcher who analyzed only eight of the Old Testament predictions about Jesus came to this conclusion: "The chance that any man might have . . . fulfilled all eight prophecies is 1 in 100,000,000,000,000,000." If we can trust the prophecies in their accuracy of factual information about Jesus' arrival on this planet, we can surely trust those prophecies when they use titles and designations to indicate that Jesus the Messiah is God.

The Claims Of The New Testament

The New Testament is Jesus' book. It begins with His family tree and ends with His future tri-

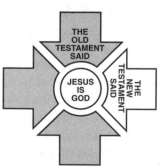

umph. In between are amazing accounts of His life, His death, His resurrection, His ascension, and His acclaim. But who is this man? Does His book really tell us? Can we trust the record? Sure He healed the sick, but was He just a first-century snake oil salesman with good connections? Sure He fed the hungry, but could He just have been a sleight-of-hand magician? Sure He wowed the masses, but could He have been no more than an ancient superstar?

To find out, we have to go behind the stories of what Jesus did. We have to find out what those people who observed Him said about Him. A biographer who writes about someone who is no longer on the scene talks to those who either knew the subject or at least knew about him from those who knew him. We too can "interview" Jesus' contemporaries to clarify our view of Jesus. Let's turn first to a man who knew Jesus well, the apostle John.

The Viewpoint Of The Apostle John. Did the apostle John actually set out to show that Jesus was God? To begin answering that question, let's turn first to the opening words of John's gospel.

> *In the beginning was the Word, and the Word was with God, and the Word was God. He was in the beginning with God. All things were made through Him, and without Him nothing was made that was made. In Him was life, and the life was the light of men (1:1-4).*

Once we understand what John meant by the term Word, it becomes difficult to read anything into this passage other than the deity of Jesus. Here, as in three other passages in the New Testament (Jn. 1:14; 1 Jn. 1:1; Rev. 19:13), the designation *Word* or *Logos* refers specifically to Jesus. That John is referring to Jesus becomes clear when we look at verse 14, where he said, "And the Word became flesh and dwelt among us." Notice in John 1:1-4 that the following characteristics of Jesus are traits that can belong only to God.

"In the beginning." Anyone in John's day who was familiar with the sacred Scriptures would have recognized his allusion to the book we now call Genesis. In that era, Genesis was commonly referred to as "In the beginning," so the reader of John's gospel would automatically think of the creation record and its assumption of God's eternality. John boldly declared that Jesus was with God before the worlds began.

"The Word was with God." This clause indicates that although Jesus was God, He was a distinct entity who had, as the preposition with implies, communion and fellowship with God the Father.

"The Word was God." Here it is: a definitive statement of Jesus' deity. This does not say that He was "a God," as some suggest. That rendering of this clause results from an unscholarly interpretation of the fact that the Greek word *theos* (God) appears here without the definite article *the*. Those who do this fail to recognize that John omitted the article to point out that Jesus is God, just like the Father is God. Had he used it, he would have implied that Jesus alone is the God. Yet those who deny the deity of Christ continue to insist on interpreting this phrase "a god."

> "There exists no documentation from the ancient world witnessed by so excellent a set of textual and historical testimonies [as the Bible]."
>
> Clark Pinnock

There are two problems with this. First, the New Testament is filled with references to God without the use of a definite article in the Greek (282 times). In fact, even the translators who render John 1:1 to read "a god" translate the exact same phrase as "God" in 94 percent of the other 281 instances. To be consistent, these should say "a god."

> "In the beginning was the Word, and the Word was with God, and the Word was God."
> John 1:1

This construction occurs 20 times in the gospel of John alone. Should John 1:18, then, be translated, "No one has seen a god at any time"?

Besides the problems with the grammar, there is another difficulty posed by this mistranslation. If indeed the verse were to be translated "a god," then we would be faced with a concept of polytheism that is totally foreign to anything in the Christian faith. If Jesus is "a god," then there must be others. Yet Scripture is clear in this matter: There is only one God. Calling Jesus "a god" among other gods would have been as unacceptable to the first-century reader as it is to the 21st-century theist. John's contemporaries were thoroughly schooled in monotheism, and any departure from that well-established doctrine would have been rejected.

"All things were made through Him." Who but God can be credited with creation? Referring again to the first verse of Genesis, we are reminded that "God created the heavens and the earth." And now John revealed Jesus as the active agent in creation. How else can this be reconciled but to conclude that Jesus the Savior is also God the Creator?

The Viewpoint Of The Apostle Paul. John wasn't alone in saying that Jesus was God. The apostle Paul also made this doctrine a strong part of his writings. Here is a sampling of verses written by Paul that attribute deity to Jesus.

Romans 9:5. *"Christ came, who is over all, the eternally blessed God."* No amount of interpretive gymnastics can deny the simple grammar of this verse that Christ is God.

Philippians 2:5-6. *"Let this mind be in you which was also in Christ Jesus, who, being in the form of God, did not consider it robbery to be equal with God."* Here we get a picture of Jesus in both of His essential natures—as God and as man. First, He had always existed as God in His essential nature. Second, He voluntarily laid aside the majesty and glory of being God to become the God-man—the humble Servant who was obedient to death. Jesus, then, was God and remained God by nature, even when He became a man on earth.

Philippians 2:10-11. *"At the name of Jesus every knee should bow, . . . every tongue should confess that Jesus Christ is Lord, to the glory of God the Father."* God would not allow anyone other than Himself to be worshiped. For Him to let people worship one lesser than He would be to violate the first commandment (see also Mt. 4:10).

1 Timothy 3:16. *"Great is the mystery of godliness: God was manifest in the flesh, justified in the Spirit, seen by angels, preached among the Gentiles, believed on in the world, received up in glory."* The God who was manifested in the flesh was Jesus, for He did all that this verse said He did.

Titus 2:13. *"Looking for the blessed hope and glorious appearing of our great God and Savior Jesus Christ."* A literal translation of the grammar of this sentence indicates that Paul was referring to only one person here: God the Son.

The Claims Of Jesus

Could the statements in the New Testament about Jesus' deity have been made by a few misguided followers? Could those writers have misread the signals? Perhaps their desire to worship someone was so strong that they developed this idea of Jesus' deity on their own. Perhaps they misunderstood Jesus' mission on earth. If they did, they sure had good company! Jesus Himself also claimed that He was God.

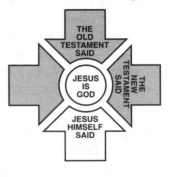

Jesus sometimes spoke in terms and phrases that left His listeners unsure as to what He meant. This can be seen in certain dialogues between Jesus and His disciples. You can imagine them walking away from some of these discussions with Jesus, scratching their heads over some hard-to-grasp concept He had just given them.

When Jesus spoke of His deity with those who were not His followers, though, they didn't reach up to scratch their head, they reached down to pick up rocks. They knew exactly what He was claiming to be. And they wanted to stone Him for it.

John 10. A good example of this is found in John 10. As Jesus walked through the temple, some Jews demanded of Him, "If you are the Christ, tell us plainly" (v.24). Jesus' reply was unmistakable in its clarity, and volatile in its message. He said:

> *I told you, and you do not believe. The works that I do in My Father's name, they bear witness of Me. But you do not believe, because you are not of My sheep, as I said to you. My sheep hear My voice, and I know them, and they follow Me. And I give them eternal life, and they shall never perish; neither shall anyone snatch them out of My hand. My Father, who has given them to Me, is greater than all; and no one is able to snatch them out of My Father's hand. I and My Father are one (vv. 25-30).*

Clearly, the Jews had a major problem with this statement. They knew that Old Testament law called for the death of anyone claiming deity. And they understood that this was exactly what Jesus was doing. They knew what He meant when He called God "My Father" and not "our" Father (v.25), claimed to be able to bestow eternal life (v.28), and said, "I and My Father are one" (v.30).

These claims of Jesus sent the Jews on a rock hunt. There was no doubt in their minds about Jesus' words. In fact, they told Jesus they were gathering ammunition because, as they said, "You, being a Man, make Yourself God" (v.33).

John 8. An earlier exchange between Jesus and a different group led to similar results. In a confrontation that must have created some high-power tension, the Jews accused Jesus of possessing a demon. In the dialogue that followed, Jesus said, "Your father Abraham rejoiced to see My day, and he saw it and was glad" (v.56). The Jews couldn't believe their ears. They wanted to know how a man who wasn't even 50 years old could have seen Abraham.

Jesus' reply was even more unsettling for His listeners. He announced, "Most assuredly, I say to you, before Abraham was, I AM" (v.58). The Jews were aghast. Jesus had just told them who He is. In using the term I AM, He undoubtedly reminded the Jews of God's statement to Moses at the burning bush in Exodus 3:14. Because of their familiarity with the Scriptures, they would have known that Jesus had declared His deity—His timelessness and His identity with Yahweh. We know they understood exactly what Jesus was saying, because He had to hide Himself and make a quick getaway to avoid being a target for their stones.

John 14. On another occasion, Jesus claimed His deity in the presence of a much friendlier crowd. While eating with the disciples, Jesus predicted Peter's denial and assured Thomas that He was "the way, the truth, and the life" (v.6). Then Philip asked Him to show them the Father. His answer is an unmistakable claim to deity. He said, "He who has seen Me has seen the Father" (v.9), and "Do you not believe that I am in the Father, and the Father in Me?" (v.10).

The Response Of Jesus' Observers

We have already seen that the Jews who listened to Jesus knew that He was claiming to be God. They weren't the only ones who got the picture. Oth-

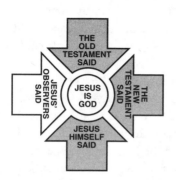

ers of varying social status and with varying degrees of interest in Jesus' ministry also heard Jesus say He was God. Their reactions, and Jesus' response to them, make an interesting study.

Matthew 21. Let's look at a conversation that occurred shortly after Jesus cleansed the temple in Jerusalem. Jesus had just come into the city to the welcome of an admiring crowd. The people continued to cry out, "Hosanna to the Son of David" (v.15). This didn't sit well with the chief priests and scribes. They thought Jesus should know better than to accept this worship. After all, wasn't He familiar with the first commandment?

Notice His response to their indignant question "Do You hear what these are saying?" (v.16). Jesus gave them more to think about than they had bargained for when He countered with this reference to Psalm 8:2, "Yes. Have you never read, 'Out of the mouth of babes and nursing infants You have perfected praise'?" (v.16). Unmistakably, Jesus was telling His listeners that these words of worship were prepared by God for worship of God. By accepting those "Hosannas," Jesus was declaring His deity.

This wasn't the only time Jesus accepted the worship of others. On at least two other occasions, He allowed His followers to give Him the praise and honor that can only go to God.

Matthew 16. The first incident occurred after Jesus asked His disciples to respond to a kind of first-century poll. They had been out talking with the people of Caesarea Philippi, which is north of the Sea of Galilee. Jesus asked, "Who do men say that I, the Son of Man, am?" (v.13). After hearing a random sampling of responses, He pointed the question directly at the Twelve, "But who do you say that I am?" (v.15).

Simon Peter, in typical boldness, declared, "You are the Christ, the Son of the living God" (v.16). Here was a perfect opportunity for Jesus to dispel this growing idea that He was something other than just a great man. But Jesus wouldn't do that. Instead, He commended Peter for his declaration. The terms that Peter used indicate that Jesus was "of the same substance" or "of the same characteristics" as God. Knowing that Peter's confession was a reference to His deity, Jesus said, "Blessed are you, Simon Bar-Jonah, for flesh and blood has not revealed this to you, but My Father who is in heaven" (v.17). Once more, Jesus willingly received the worship of man.

> "For it is written, 'You shall worship the Lord your God, and Him only you shall serve.' . . . And when they saw [Jesus], they worshiped Him."
>
> Matthew 4:10; 28:17

John 20. A second dialogue between Jesus and one of His disciples demonstrates in even more specific terms Jesus' willingness to consider Himself worthy of worship. It happened more than a week after Jesus had risen from the dead. All of the disciples but one, Thomas, had seen Jesus. All the talk in the world was not going to convince him that Jesus was alive. He had to see the Savior for himself.

As he and the others were assembled together early in the second week after the resurrection, Jesus suddenly appeared among them. He requested that Thomas touch Him so he would know for sure that this was Jesus in the flesh. Apparently Thomas did so, for he responded, "My Lord and my God!" (v.28). With these words, Thomas summarized the deity of Christ as both Lord and God. And as Jesus did with Peter, He commended Thomas for not doubting that He was God.

> "I saw one of his heads as if it had been mortally wounded, and his deadly wound was healed. And all the world marveled and followed the beast."
> Revelation 13:3

Not much has changed in 2,000 years. Those who choose not to accept the claims of Jesus react in rock-hurling rage at the suggestion that Jesus is God. Conversely, those who know Him personally and see Him for who He is react with undivided devotion and praise to the Man who is God.

But What About These Verses?

The various opinions that people hold about Jesus can be put into at least two categories of belief. First, there are those who use no source other than their own imagination to explain who they think Jesus might be. Their opinions can range from the wildly ridiculous (like saying He was from another planet) to the fairly logical (like saying He was just a great moral teacher). But they are never solidly biblical. People in this category seem to be willing to accept the biblical record when it tells us of Jesus' love for people, mercy on the sick, and wisdom for the masses, but they reject the Bible when its message suggests that Jesus was God.

The other group is made up of "religious" people who claim to use the Bible as their guide, yet have come to a conclusion that is different from that of orthodox Christianity. The various cults are in this category. These people truly feel that they are correct when they conclude that the Bible does not support the contention that Jesus is God. Let's look at some of the verses these people use either to support their case or to try to disprove the doctrine of Christ's deity.

John 14:28. *"If you loved Me, you would rejoice because I said, I am going to the Father, for My Father is greater than I."* This verse has been used by some groups to "prove" that Jesus was second in command to God. They wonder how Jesus can be God if God is greater than He.

An explanation of this begins with a look at Paul's teaching in Philippians 2:5-8. Paul said:

Let this mind be in you which was also in Christ Jesus, who, being in the form of God, did not consider it robbery to be equal with God, but made Himself of no reputation, taking the form of a servant, and coming in the likeness of men. And being found in appearance as a man, He humbled Himself and became obedient to the point of death, even the death of the cross.

Jesus chose to set aside some of His attributes to become the God-man. He chose to subordinate Himself—not only to God the Father but also to man. This is not a commentary on His nature, which of course no one can change, but on His purpose—His office—while on earth. Just as no one could conclude that Jesus became less than man because He chose to become man's servant (see Mk. 10:45), so no one should conclude that Jesus was less than God because He subjected Himself to the Father while on earth. John 14:28 does not disprove Jesus' claim to be God. Rather, it shows His willing submission to His Father during His 33 years among men.

> Just as no one could conclude that Jesus became less than man by choosing to become man's servant, so no one should conclude that Jesus was less than God because He subjected Himself to the Father while on earth.

Revelation 3:14. *"To the angel of the church of the Laodiceans write, 'These things says the Amen, the Faithful and True Witness, the Beginning of the creation of God.'"* The "Amen" of this verse is obviously Jesus

Christ. But with that fact established, those who believe in the deity of Christ begin to part ways with those who don't. Those who don't think Jesus is God contend that the phrase, "the Beginning of the creation of God" clearly points out that Jesus was the first created being formed by God. That assumption alone would be death for a "Jesus is God" theology, for how could someone who is not eternal be the eternal God? Let's investigate this theory and see if it holds up.

First, a comment on the translation of the phrase is essential. The Greek literally reads, "the Beginning of the creation of God." The grammatical construction in the Greek makes it impossible to translate it "by God."

Second, the Greek word for beginning (*arche*) implies the active role of creating—not the inactive role of being created. Jesus, then, is the Beginner of God's creation, not the first created being. This proper interpretation of the text harmonizes with other Scripture verses that tell us of Christ's deity and of His role as Creator.

> Jesus is clearly different from the creation because He was involved in the creation. The Creator cannot create Himself.

Colossians 1:15. *"He is the image of the invisible God, the firstborn over all creation."* Everybody knows what a firstborn is. He's the baby born first—the one with the birthrights. Well, sometimes that's what it means. But like many words, it can also mean something else. It can also denote rank, position, or privilege. Look for instance at Paul's statement just three verses later: "He is the head of the body, the church, who is the beginning, the firstborn from the dead." Obviously, the word *firstborn* takes on a figurative meaning here. Likewise, in Hebrews 12:23 it is used to speak of something far different from the birth of the first child in a family.

But that would still leave us with only the possibility—not the certainty—that the word *firstborn* means superiority. If all else were equal, either interpretation would be acceptable. But there are other considerations. Notably, there are two verses in the same chapter of Colossians that present a powerful commentary. In Colossians 1:16-17, Paul said in reference to Jesus, "All things were created through Him and for Him. And He is before all things, and in Him all things consist." Here Paul drew a clear line of demarcation between the created and the Creator. Jesus is clearly different from the creation because He was involved in the creation. The Creator cannot create Himself.

John 10:34. *"Jesus answered them, 'Is it not written in your law, "I said, 'You are gods'"?'"* This verse causes quite a stir from those who don't want to believe that Jesus represented deity. "So what if Jesus said He was God?" they ask. "There are lots of gods. Jesus even called His enemies gods. Therefore, if there is enough room in Jesus' theology for gods who aren't even on His side, being a god isn't so exclusive."

That kind of thinking, though logical on the surface, does not reflect the intent of Jesus' words in John 10. His statement was a quote of Psalm 82:6, in which God is depicted as entering an assembly of judges to condemn their unfair treatment of others. The word translated "gods" means "mighty ones," or in this case, "judges."

Jesus used this rather unusual quote as part of an argument to reveal the hypocrisy of His enemies. They didn't protest the statement by Asaph that referred to human judges as "gods," yet they denounced this Sinless One when He claimed the title "Son of God."

Helping You Help Others

The following questions are listed here for you to use in teaching or discipling others. We suggest that these questions be discussed prior to studying the specific section in the booklet—as preview questions.

Claims Of The Old Testament

1. What is the value of Old Testament prophecies that talk of Jesus' deity?
2. What would it do to your view of Christ if there were no Old Testament prophecies about Him?
3. What specific details about Christ do you think would be important in a prophecy to make it useful as proof of His deity?

Claims Of The New Testament

1. Why would it be important for the people who were Jesus' contemporaries to say that He was God?
2. What does John 1:1-4 tell us about Jesus?
3. What verses in the New Testament besides John 1:1-4 would you use to support Jesus deity?

Claims Of Jesus

1. What is so vital about Jesus' own declarations that He is God?
2. When Jesus made His claims to deity, did the people to whom He spoke know what He was saying?
3. What kinds of things did Jesus do that demonstrated His deity?

Be Careful What You Call Him

Let's suppose you are browsing through a bookstore and you find a book on integrity. You leaf through the table of contents, scan a few pages, peek at the last chapter, and decide that this would be a valuable addition to your library. You pay the $18.95, take the book home, and begin plowing through it. Fascinated by this author's insights, you begin taking notes, eager to learn all you can about integrity so you can increase your own level of honesty and trustworthiness—something nobody ever has too much of.

Obviously the writer knows his subject, so it occurs to you that you should find out a little about him. You turn to the book jacket and begin reading. It says something like this, "The author, who claims to be the most intelligent person alive, thinks he is the king of the United States. Having come to this planet from a faraway galaxy, the author enjoys painting masterpieces, writing classics, and making billion-dollar real estate deals in his spare time."

Slamming the book shut, you would either rush back to the store for a refund or make a beeline for the nearest trash can. Having discovered what this author thinks about himself, you would no longer trust a word he said. His words about integrity and honesty would be as valuable as a Yogi Berra dissertation on nuclear physics.

What does this fanciful story have to do with Jesus Christ? It illustrates how we would have to react to the Bible if Jesus were not God. It shows the incredulity we would express toward the story of Jesus if He were not indeed the God-man. It demonstrates mankind's need to verify a person's words by checking them against his character. If we can't trust a person's character, it is impossible to trust his words. Likewise, the truthfulness and integrity of character is verified by trustworthy words.

As we apply this test to Jesus, we must review a couple of factors. First, Jesus' life and teachings are models of integrity and goodness. This fact is recognized almost universally. His acts of healing the infirm, raising the dead, and demonstrating gentle love match His teachings on kindness, compassion, and morality. It can be concluded, then, that Jesus is a moral, trustworthy Person.

The second factor to consider is that Jesus claimed to be equal with God, to be God's Son, to be God. These claims were verified by the words and actions of His followers and contested by the words and actions of His enemies.

These two factors leave us with only three reasonable options about who Jesus is.

1. A Deluded Lunatic

If Jesus is not God, then He could be accused of having delusions of grandeur. Yet those who knew Him best recognized that Jesus' claim to deity was not outlandish. They knew that it corresponded perfectly to who He showed them He was.

2. A Great Liar

If Jesus is not God, then He could have just been lying. In this case, He would have had to know that

He was not who He was claiming to be. This becomes increasingly difficult to accept the more one looks at His life. How could He, in every other instance, convey the essence of honesty and credibility if on this one major point He continued to lie? How could He deceive so many godly people if He were doing such an ungodly thing? How could One so seemingly moral be such a great liar?

3. God

What Jesus said and what He did most closely support this option. Jesus fulfilled the prophecies about the One who would be God on earth. He manifested the attributes of the eternal God. Sinful men found Him to be sinless. He knew the Scriptures as no one else did. He did things only God could do.

A lunatic can claim anything, but he can't deliver on his claims. Jesus did. A liar can play amazing mental games with people, but he can't prove anything he says. Jesus, though, was born where the God-man was to be born, lived as the God-man should live, died as the God-man was to die, and lived again as only the God-man could live again.

What do you call Jesus? You have only the three options. But be careful. Calling Him anything but God will put your eternal soul in serious jeopardy. Only when you recognize that Jesus is God can you see Him as the source of life. Only as you trust all of God's Word—not just in regard to Jesus' life but also in regard to His deity—will you understand the importance of His death. Be careful what you call Jesus. Your eternal life depends on it.

What You Can't Say

From *Mere Christianity* by C. S. Lewis

I am trying here to prevent anyone saying the really foolish thing that people often say about Him: "I'm ready to accept Jesus as a great moral teacher, but I don't accept His claim to be God." That is the one thing we must not say. A man who was merely a man and said the sort of things Jesus said would not be a great moral teacher. He would either be a lunatic—on the level with the man who says he is a poached egg—or else he would be the devil of hell. You must make your choice. Either this man was, and is, the Son of God—or else a madman or something worse. You can shut Him up for a fool, you can spit at Him and kill Him as a demon; or you can fall at His feet and call Him Lord and God. But let us not come with any patronizing nonsense about His being a great human teacher. He has not left that open to us.

We are faced, then, with a frightening alternative. This man we are talking about either was (and is) just what He said or else a lunatic, or something worse. Now it seems to me obvious that He was neither a lunatic nor a fiend; and consequently, however strange or terrifying or unlikely it may seem, I have to accept the view that He was and is God.

What Do *You* Say?

The question you must answer is a simple one. It's not, "What do you think of a certain religion?"

It's not, "What do you think of Christians?"

It's not, "What good works have you done lately?"

It's not, "What are the traditions of your church?"

The question that stands between every human and God is this: "What are you going to do with Jesus?"

Jesus said, "I am the way, the truth, and the life. No one comes to the Father except through Me" (Jn. 14:6). Paul and Silas said, "Believe on the Lord Jesus Christ, and you will be saved" (Acts 16:31). Luke wrote, "Nor is there salvation in any other, for there is no other name under heaven given among men by which we must be saved" (Acts 4:12). And Paul said that "God was in Christ reconciling the world to Himself" (2 Cor. 5:19).

The message is clear: Faith in Jesus is the only way to God. So what are you going to do with Him? Will you allow a philosopher's deceiving words to make you mistrust the Savior? Will you permit a translator's trick to cause you to reject Jesus? Will you let the musings of mere humans carry more weight than the message of Almighty God?

Please don't. Take Jesus at His word. Put your faith in His sacrifice for your sins on the cross of Calvary. You'll find the joy that comes from being set free from the penalty of sin. What will you do with Jesus? That's the most important question you will ever answer.

3

Why Did Christ Have To Die?

Couldn't Christ have accomplished more by living a full and happy life? Think of the people He could have healed, the teaching He could have done, the problems He could have solved. Why was He obsessed with dying? Why didn't He defend Himself in court for the sake of His family, His disciples, and all who admired Him?

This booklet, compiled by our staff of writers, takes a look at the reasons given in the Bible why Christ planned and allowed His own death.

Martin R. De Haan II

The Symbol Of The Cross

Can you imagine what public reaction would be if a fundamentalist religious group adopted an electric chair as its symbol? Think of what it would be like to see an image of an electric chair on top of their meeting places or as jewelry hanging around their necks.

Yet that's what the cross amounts to. The cross was a means of capital punishment. Crucifixion was the way the Romans put their worst criminals to death. It was horrible—far worse than a gas chamber, firing squad, or even a hangman's noose.

The cross has become so widely used as religious jewelry that it has lost much of its original meaning and horror.

Why, then, do Christians make so much of this instrument of public ridicule and torture? Why are Christians obsessed with this symbol of death? Do they realize what they are doing?

In many cases, the answer seems to be no. Even Christians fail to realize the implications of the cross. It has become so widely used as religious jewelry, as a symbol of love and hope, and even as a sign of good luck that it has lost much of its original meaning and horror. It has become so generally accepted, in fact, that everyone from devoted followers of Christ to hard-rock musicians wear its image around their necks.

The Opinions Of The Cross

So what do people think of the cross? More specifically, what do they think of the cross as it relates to Christ? That's where the symbol comes from, and that's where the real discussion begins. Why did a beautiful life have to come to such a terrible end? What was in His mind? What should now be in ours? Here are some of the explanations people give for the death of Christ.

"It's an example of nonresistance." Some people feel that when Jesus died on the cross He was giving us the ultimate example of how to live in a violent, hostile world. They say that His death shows us how to live successfully by being strong enough to let others have their way.

> "Father, forgive them, for they do not know what they do."
> Jesus, from the cross

"It means whatever you want it to mean." Those who take this approach generally believe that Christ did not actually accomplish anything when He died on the cross. Since it has become such a part of our awareness, it can be used to symbolize many different things.

"It has no real meaning." Some people say that the significance of Christ was in His life—not in His death. They believe that He came to live a flawless life on earth so that we could know what God is like. But that was all God sent Him to do. His death, they say, was not related to His mission on earth.

"It represents failure." Those who hold this view say that Jesus had a noble and global plan for earth, but that He died before He could carry it out. His mission was aborted when the Roman soldiers nailed Him to the cross like a common criminal. When Christ died, these people say, it meant that He had failed.

The Offensiveness Of The Cross

Some people see so much good in the cross that they fail to see it as a terrible instrument of death. But to others, the cross is so offensive that they fail to see its value.

The apostle Paul said it would be that way. Writing to the Christians at Corinth, he said:

We preach Christ crucified, to the Jews a stumbling block and to the Greeks foolishness (1 Cor. 1:23).

The apostles' claim that Jesus was the long-awaited Messiah was almost impossible for a Jew to accept. To believe that the Messiah died on the cross was unimaginable—especially since the Old Testament said that anyone who died on a tree was cursed by God (Dt. 21:23). The cross offended them deeply.

> "The message of the cross is foolishness to those who are perishing."
> 1 Corinthians 1:18

The Gentiles too were offended by the cross. In their opinion, it was foolishness. They felt that their logical thinking and good living would satisfy the gods. They saw no reason to believe in the senseless death of an obscure Galilean.

And what about people today? Does the cross still offend? Do people still stumble over its simple message?

- If their philosophical point of view does not include the reality of sin and the need of a Savior, the answer is yes!
- If by their godly living and high morals they expect to win God's approval, yes!
- If they expect His favor because of their national heritage or family name, yes!
- If they think God is too loving to punish people for their wrongs, yes!

The message of the cross, a first-century "electric chair," will offend them.

What we need to realize, however, is that the cross is not just something hard to live with. It actually makes life possible. In fact, the cross resolved the greatest dilemma of all time.

The Dilemma Of The Cross

The cross resolves two great dilemmas—one from God's perspective and one from man's. All parents can understand the dilemma of not wanting to correct a disobedient child with painful discipline, while at the same time realizing that you can't just blink or yawn at his bad behavior.

What do you do? You love that little one. But he has also clearly disobeyed you, and right now he is lying to you in an attempt to cover it up. Sure, you love him. But you also know that you can't just brush off the problem. He has to be punished—and you've got to do it.

The situation caused by our sin was infinitely more

complex than that. But there are some parallels. Because God is a holy God, He cannot just ignore our sin. Yet because He is a loving God, He is not merely willing to let us get what we deserve.

Another illustration might help us to see the dilemma from man's perspective. Imagine a group of people trapped on the roof of a high-rise building engulfed in flames. The only way to safety is to jump to the roof of an adjoining building—30 feet away! In desperation, people begin to attempt the impossible leap. Some jump farther out than others, but all fall to their death.

So it is with man's helpless condition before God. Our sin caused a separation between us and a holy God that cannot be bridged by anything we do. We are utterly helpless to save ourselves. But the love of God provided a way: the cross of Christ.

We might diagram the dilemma like this:

Holy	GOD	Loving
Sinful	MAN	Helpless

The necessity for Calvary's tree can be traced back to a much earlier tree. All our problems began when our first parents willfully and disobediently ate of the tree of the knowledge of good and evil. God had said that Adam and his wife would die if they ate the fruit of that tree. And they did. From that time on, no man was the man he was created to be. From that time on, the children of Adam were born physically alive but spiritually dead. Not only was the garden paradise lost, but so was the innocence man was created with.

Every child born from Eden until today has proven that innocence was lost. Once created to walk with God, man has inherited a nature that causes him to forget God, to hate his fellowmen, and to live a life of self-destruction. Because of this, David the king of Israel went on record as saying, "Behold, I was brought forth in iniquity, and in sin my mother conceived me" (Ps. 51:5).

> Our sin caused a separation between us and a holy God that cannot be bridged by anything we do.

And the apostle Paul wrote, "Through one man sin entered the world, and death through sin" (Rom. 5:12) and "the wages of sin is death" (6:23). In another letter he wrote, "In Adam all die" (1 Cor. 15:22).

This is our condition. When Adam followed the way of the serpent, he didn't just hurt himself. When he ate of that tree in defiance of his Maker, spiritual and physical death fell upon all men. And so it has come now to us. The proof is, all of us sinned against God the first chance we got.

Furthermore, we can't do anything to help ourselves. No amount of self-improvement or good deeds can win back what Adam lost. The prophet Isaiah saw this clearly, for he said that our best efforts are nothing better than dirty rags (Is. 64:6). Much later, the apostle Paul expressed the same awareness (Eph. 2:8-9). His words remind us that no man can pull himself up to God by yanking on his own bootstraps.

This is bad news. But the Bible, the most reliable book in the world, claims to be true. We are born into this world spiritually dead. We are born separated from God. We are born into a world of physical and spiritual death, and unless something happens, we will live out our lives in rebellion against God. Unless something happens, we are destined for the judgment of God—the second death, the lake of fire created for the devil and all of his demons.

And if that were not enough, the Bible tells us that there's not a thing in the world we can do on our own to merit a rescue. Without a doubt, we need help. We need rescue. We need to be delivered from our guilt and bondage—before it is everlastingly too late.

The Resolution Of The Cross

When Adam and Eve sinned, God could have struck them dead instantly. And He would have been just in doing so, because His holy nature demands that disobedience be punished by death.

Yet, because God is love, He did not strike our first parents dead. Instead, He sought them out, provided them with a covering of animal skins, and gave to them a wonderful promise (Gen. 3:15). At that point God announced the good news. Yes, the good news is that God Himself resolved the dilemma—His holiness is counter-balanced by His love! Love found a way. Love found another tree, the cross (Rom. 5:6). God in

Holy	GOD	Loving
	CHRIST	
Sinful	MAN	Helpless

His wisdom provided a way to undo the terrible damage done to man at that first tree.

The tree in the Garden of Eden has now given way to the cross. And on that tree of humiliation, goodness triumphed over evil. Mercy triumphed over justice. The rescue was completed. The mission was accomplished. The dilemma was resolved.

The Principles Of The Cross

How did God do it? What did He see in that ugly tree of execution? What happened as His only begotten and dearly loved Son bled, struggled, cried,

"It is finished," and then gave up His spirit?

Let's look at two principles of resolution that ended the dilemma caused by our sin and helplessness and God's holiness and love: (1) the principle of adequate sacrifice, and (2) the principle of necessary substitution.

PRINCIPLE 1:
The cross provided an adequate sacrifice.

There can be no forgiveness without a sacrificial death (Heb. 9:22). Through His death on the cross, Jesus

Holy	GOD	Loving
Sacrifice	CHRIST	Sacrifice
Sinful	MAN	Helpless

Christ presented to God a sacrifice sufficient to pay for the sins of all mankind. The animal deaths of Old Testament days fell far short of that, for they did not actually take away sin.

The Old Testament sacrifices had to be offered every day. Animal after animal was brought to the altar and slain. Each new day brought a new round of sacrificial slayings. The writer of Hebrews, commenting on this fact, said, "It is not possible that the blood of bulls and goats could take away sins" (Heb. 10:4).

Furthermore, those sacrifices were only for sins committed involuntarily, in ignorance, or through human weakness (Lev. 4:2-7). A sacrifice could not be given for a premeditated, deliberate sin in Old Testament days. That is why David, when he repented of his double sin of adultery with Bathsheba and the murder of Uriah, did not even present a sacrifice. Rather, he came before God with "a broken and contrite heart" to find forgiveness (Ps. 51:16-17).

By His death on the cross, the Lord Jesus provided a once-for-all sacrifice for all our sins (Heb. 10:12). He was the complete and perfect sacrifice. It satisfied every demand of a holy God, and it brings salvation to all who trust in Christ.

Christ's sacrifice was adequate for several reasons:

- *He became a member of the human family.* He could truly represent us (something no angel could do) because He took to Himself a human nature.
- *He lived a sinless life.* Confronted by physical, mental, and spiritual temptation, Jesus did not sin (Heb. 4:15). Therefore, when He died, He did so as a perfect human being. Because He did not sin, He could die for our sins.
- *He remained God.* Even though Christ became fully human, He also retained His full deity. He was not half God and half man; He was fully God and fully man. His goodness is what gave His sacrifice infinite value, making it adequate to pay for the sins of all mankind.

PRINCIPLE 2:
The cross provided a necessary substitute.

Jesus had substitution in mind when He told His followers that He would give His life as a "ransom for many" (Mk. 10:45).

Holy	GOD	Loving
Substitute	CHRIST	Substitute
Sinful	MAN	Helpless

Whether they recognized it or not when He said it, His disciples would soon learn that Christ was planning to give His life in exchange for their legal release from sin and guilt. On the cross, Christ would die in their place—and in our place. At Calvary, He died the death all of us should have died, taking the punishment we deserved. "For God so loved the world that He gave His only begotten Son" (Jn. 3:16). Because of our helplessness, God in love sent His Son to be our substitute. He exchanged His life for ours, dying that we might live (Isa. 53:5-6; Rom. 5:8; 1 Cor. 15:3; 2 Cor. 5:21; 1 Pet. 2:24; 3:18).

When Jesus said that He had come to give His life a ransom for many, His hearers probably realized that He had in mind the Jewish sacrificial system. From early childhood they had seen sheep or oxen or turtle doves brought to the altar and killed. They knew that the animal's death was associated with their sins. As they watched the priest place his hand on the forehead of the animal, they realized that this was a symbol of the transfer of guilt from the sinner to the animal. Then, when they saw the beast killed and the blood sprinkled around the altar, they understood that this blood in some way symbolized the taking away of their guilt.

> Christ overcame our inability to save ourselves by paying the price for our sins.

The same principle of the substitute was later fulfilled in the One of whom John the Baptist said, "Behold! The Lamb of God who takes away the sin of the world!" (Jn. 1:29).

This principle is illustrated by a story from American history. In a tribe of Indians, someone was stealing chickens. The chief declared that, if caught, the offender would receive 10 lashes. When the stealing continued, he raised it to 20 lashes. Still the chickens methodically disappeared. In anger the chief raised the sentence to 100 lashes—a sure sentence of death.

The thief was finally caught. But the chief faced a terrible dilemma. The thief was his own mother!

When the day of penalty came, the whole tribe gathered. Would the chief's love override his justice? The crowd gasped when he ordered his mother to be tied to the whipping post. The chief removed his shirt, revealing his powerful stature, and took the whip in hand. But instead of raising it to strike the first blow, he handed it to a strong, young brave at his side.

Slowly the chief walked over to his mother and wrapped his massive arms around her in an engulfing embrace. Then he ordered the brave to give him the 100 lashes.

That's what Jesus did for us. In love He became our substitute and died in our place. He overcame our inability to save ourselves by paying the price for our sins. In our illustration, a mother's life was extended by the substitutionary love of her son; for us, everlasting life was bought through the substitutionary death of Christ.

The death of Christ, therefore, was of tremendous value, for it bridged the gulf between God and man. Look again at what happened.

Man's Condition: Condemned by Adam's sin and his own, and powerless to do anything to save himself, man was under the penalty of death.

God's Position: God was bound by His own holiness to punish evil. To do less would be to violate His own character. But because He is also love, He desired to save man from his sentence of death.

Holy	GOD	Loving
Sacrifice Substitute	CHRIST	Sacrifice Substitute
Sinful	MAN	Helpless

The Resolution: Christ, God's Son, became human, lived a sinless life, then died on our behalf. His sacrificial, substitutionary death made possible our salvation.

Look at the complete diagram. It shows you how the death of Christ resolved the dilemma.

The Results Of The Cross

The death of Jesus Christ 2,000 years ago was not just a heroic act that caught the imagination of a band of religious idealists. Nor was it an act of weakness.

It was a loving, courageous, death-defying mission of rescue. The result is that the person who trusts in Jesus Christ is changed in his relationship to God. He is changed in his relationship to his own sin. And his future is changed, both for this life and the life to come.

That change is spelled out in four basic concepts that show the results of what Christ did for us. Here is what is ours once we have accepted the sacrificial, substitutionary death of Christ.

1. RECONCILIATION:
We are at peace with God. When Jesus Christ died on the cross, He made it possible for us to be reconciled to God and restored to fellowship with Him by faith in Christ. Enmity is turned to friendship, alienation to sonship, hostility to faith, and hatred to love because of Christ's sacrifice on the cross (Rom. 5:1,10; 2 Cor. 5:18-20; Eph. 2:16; Col. 1:20-22).

2. JUSTIFICATION:
We are declared right before God. When Jesus Christ died, He absorbed our punishment. Therefore, when we believe in Him, our sins are no longer held against us (Rom. 3:24; 4:5; 5:1,9; 8:30-31; Ti. 3:4-7).

3. REDEMPTION:
We are ransomed from our sin and condemnation. The death of Christ also means we have been bought out of bondage to sin and Satan. The ransom price for our sin has been paid in full (Mt. 20:28; Rom. 3:24; 1 Cor. 1:30; Gal. 3:13; 4:4-5; Eph. 1:7; Col. 1:14; Ti. 2:14; Heb. 9:12; 1 Pet. 1:18-19).

4. PROPITIATION:
We are free from God's wrath. This is possible because an acceptable offering has been made on our behalf. The offering has been made to appease God, to turn His wrath from us (Rom. 3:25; Heb. 2:17; 1 Jn. 2:2; 4:10).

The Irony Of The Cross

The irony of all this is that something as ugly as the cross—something revolting enough to cause people to reject the best Man who ever lived—is actually our only hope of rescue from our spiritual helplessness. That's what the Bible says. And that's what Christ confirmed when He rose triumphantly from the dead.

The cross was not a mistake. It wasn't a good life falling on bad times. The irony of the cross is that

(1) it is the greatest example of God's love, and that (2) in dying, Christ also showed us how to live. The first point of irony is this:

Christ's Death Demonstrated God's Love.
The great truth of the most familiar and best-loved verse of the Bible is that the cross was evidence of God's love.

> *For God so loved the world that He gave His only begotten Son, that whoever believes in Him should not perish but have everlasting life (Jn. 3:16).*

A parallel passage reads, "By this we know love, because He laid down His life for us" (1 Jn. 3:16).

Some people look for God's love in nature. But they won't find it guaranteed there, because the message of the created world gives conflicting messages. Sometimes it seems to tell us that God is wonderfully loving. The warm sunshine, the gentle rain, the blooming flowers of the fields, and the watchful care of a cow for her calf all seem to say, "God is love."

At other times, however, the message of nature is quite the opposite. Sun and drought make the ground hard and unproductive. A killer tornado may roar out of a darkened sky without warning. A nest of young rabbits may be killed by a nightstalking cat or foraging jackal. Or an erupting volcano

In the cross, we see God's love at its best and our sin at its worst.

may wipe out entire villages, killing hundreds and making thousands homeless. No, the love of God cannot always be seen in nature.

Nor is God's love clearly evident in history. A family of immigrants to the United States from Vietnam or Korea may say that coming to the USA proved to them that God loves them. But if you talk to the young mother of three children whose husband was just killed by airplane hijackers, she may scoff bitterly at the idea that a loving God controls all events. Many of the Jewish people who lived through the horrors of Auschwitz or Dachau would also reject the idea that God's love is demonstrated in history.

When Christians talk about God's love being made known, therefore, they must point to something else as evidence. According to the Bible, that evidence is the cross. Because Jesus Christ is God's Son, His death was a profound declaration of God's love.

God has shown His love for us—but at great cost. In the person of Jesus Christ, God became a member of the human family. He lived His whole life without sin. Then, though innocent Himself, He died a terrible death to make our salvation possible. Shining through the darkness that surrounded Calvary that fateful day was the wondrous brilliance of the love of God. Think for a moment about what Christ suffered, and remember that it was for us.

> Because Jesus Christ is God's Son, His death was a profound declaration of God's love.

Stand in awe as He agonizes before God the Father in Gethsemane until His sweat becomes like great drops of blood falling to the ground.

Follow in horror as He is arrested like a criminal, mutilated by a Roman whip, and tortured, mocked, and derided with a crown of thorns.

Weep for Him as He stumbles under the heavy wooden beam He is forced to carry to His place of execution.

Cringe in revulsion as hardened Roman soldiers pound spikes through His hands, drive nails through His feet, and roughly drop the beam into place.

Listen to Him as He hangs there on the cross, praying for His enemies, talking lovingly to His mother, and promising salvation to the criminal who repents.

Be still as you see the sky grow black at noon, and as you sit through the 3 hours of eerie midday darkness.

Listen to His cry of abandonment, "My God, My God, why have You forsaken Me?"

Remember that on the cross, Jesus endured the agony of hell for you and me. God was His Father. He had existed with Him from all eternity in a relationship closer than anything we could ever know. Yet the Father "made Him who knew no sin to be sin for us, that we might become the righteousness of God in Him" (2 Cor. 5:21).

The second point of irony is:

Christ's Death Showed Us How To Live.
Not only did the cross give us the highest evidence of God's love, but it also provided us with a spiritual principle of life. The love that led Jesus Christ to this unparalleled deed of self-sacrifice was an example for us.

We are to love as He loved; to live as He lived. The

Lord Jesus had the cross in mind the evening before His crucifixion when He told His disciples, "A new commandment I give to you, that you love one another; as I have loved you, that you also love one another" (Jn. 13:34). Calvary love is to be standard for our love.

Jesus Christ also had His death on the cross in view when He said this:

> *Unless a grain of wheat falls into the ground and dies, it remains alone; but if it dies, it produces much grain. He who loves his life will lose it, and he who hates his life in this world will keep it for eternal life. If anyone serves Me, let him follow Me (Jn. 12:24-26).*

This is the law of the harvest: A seed must die before it can produce a plant. Jesus Christ was the "seed" that had to die. Yet His death produced spiritual life for all who would trust Him. We are the fruit of His suffering and death.

But the law of death to bring life did not end with Christ's cross. Jesus declared that it also applies to His followers. We must take the way of the cross, the way of dying to our own selfish desires, if we are to bear the kind of fruit that God created us to produce (Eph. 2:8-10).

> "Christ also suffered for us, leaving us an example, that you should follow His steps."
> 1 Peter 2:21

The apostle Paul saw this principle in Christ's death. Time and again he spoke of being crucified with Christ, of dying to self, and of walking the Calvary road. With deep conviction he wrote, "But God forbid that I should glory except in the cross of our Lord Jesus Christ, by whom the world has been crucified to me, and I to the world" (Gal. 6:14).

Because the cross of Christ was Paul's inspiration and confidence, he could write off the world-system as something useless and dead. He saw nothing in it to attract him.

When we live by the law of the harvest, we will be fruitful in our service for Christ. Following His example, we must first die to self. As we do, we will be able to say with Paul, "I have been crucified with Christ; it is no longer I who live, but Christ lives in me; and the life which I now live in the flesh I live by faith in the Son of God, who loved me and gave Himself for me" (Gal. 2:20).

> "I have been crucified with Christ; it is no longer I who live, but Christ lives in me; and the life which I now live in the flesh I live by faith in the Son of God, who loved me and gave Himself for me."
>
> The Apostle Paul
> Galatians 2:20

Here again is the irony of the cross. Not only does it bring God's life to us, but it brings our life to God.

The Background Of The Cross

We are fortunate to be able to look back to the cross and see it in perspective. The first disciples of Christ were not so privileged. For them the crucifixion came as a terrible, heart-rending tragedy. Their beloved Leader was dead. Their hopes of a messianic kingdom had evaporated. Their enemies were cheering. They were stunned by the unexpected twist of events. Only later, when Christ surprised them with His resurrected presence, did the disciples begin to understand that the Old Testament pointed to a cross as well as to a kingdom. Only then did they begin to see that Christ had to fulfill the picture of a suffering Servant before He could return as the promised King.

The resurrected Jesus explained to His astonished followers how the cross was part of the plan of God. First, He showed them His wounds. Then He said, "These are the words which I spoke to you while I was still with you, that all things must be fulfilled which were written in the Law of Moses and the Prophets and the Psalms concerning Me" (Lk. 24:44). He opened their minds to the Old Testament pictures and prophecies about His death (v.45). For example:

Old Testament Prophecies Of Christ's Death
- Genesis 3:15—The Seed of woman "bruised"
- Psalm 16:10—Messiah not left in the grave
- Psalm 22:1—Messiah's cry of forsakenness
- Psalm 22:6-8—Messiah mocked
- Psalm 22:15—Messiah's thirst
- Psalm 22:16—Messiah's pierced hands and feet
- Psalm 22:17—The stares of Messiah's enemies
- Psalm 22:18—Gambling for Messiah's garments
- Psalm 69:21—Vinegar offered to Messiah
- Isaiah 49:7—God's Servant despised
- Isaiah 50:6—Messiah physically abused
- Isaiah 52:14—Messiah's face disfigured
- Isaiah 53:5—Messiah pierced for our sins
- Isaiah 53:7—Messiah silent before His accusers
- Isaiah 53:9—Messiah's grave among the rich

- Isaiah 53:12—Messiah identified with criminals
- Daniel 9:26—God's Messiah "cut off"
- Zechariah 12:10—Messiah "pierced" by Israel
- Zechariah 13:7—The Shepherd struck down

Old Testament Pictures Of Christ's Death

The imagery of the cross appears in three Old Testament pictures.

Sacrifices. The substitutionary death of Christ is most often pictured in the Old Testament by the sacrificial system. The provision of animal skins for Adam and Eve is seen by many Bible scholars as God's initiative to provide for man's sin by means of sacrifice (Gen. 3:21). The Passover sacrifice is a primary image of deliverance through the shed blood of a lamb (Ex. 12; Lev. 23; 1 Cor. 5:7; 1 Pet. 1:19). John the Baptist connected the animal sacrifice and Jesus Christ when he cried, "Behold! The Lamb of God who takes away the sin of the world!" (Jn. 1:29). An extensive explanation is given in Hebrews 9:11–10:18.

> "Behold! The Lamb of God who takes away the sin of the world!"
>
> John 1:29

The Bronze Serpent. Israel was afflicted with the bites of serpents because of their disobedience. At God's instruction, a serpent was made out of bronze and placed on a pole in the center of camp. All who looked at it were healed of their bites (Num. 21:4-9).

Christ would be "lifted up" and all who looked on Him in faith would experience spiritual healing (Jn. 3:14-15).

Jonah. Jesus taught that the experience of Jonah in the belly of the great fish for 3 days and 3 nights was a picture of His own death, burial, and resurrection (Mt. 12:39-41).

By prophecies and pictures, therefore, the Old Testament looked forward to the death of Christ. His crucifixion was not an unforeseen detour in the plan of God. Rather, it was the reason that He came.

The Words Of The Cross

Even in dying, Christ was teaching us how to live. The seven recorded statements from the cross give us seven profound lessons on life.

1 *"Father, forgive them, for they do not know what they do"* (Lk. 23:34). Forgiveness is better than revenge.

2 *"Assuredly, I say to you, today you will be with Me in Paradise"* (Lk. 23:43). Faith is rewarded with promise.

3 *"Woman, behold your son! . . . Behold your mother!"*
(Jn. 19:26-27). Our own needs should not overshadow the needs of others.

4 *"My God, My God, why have You forsaken Me?"* (Mk. 15:34). Anything that could jeopardize our relationship with God should produce anguish.

5 *"I thirst"* (Jn. 19:28). These words, spoken to fulfill prophecy, remind us of the authority of Scripture.

6 *"It is finished"* (Jn. 19:30). Do not let yourself lose sight of your goal of doing God's will.

7 *"Father, into Your hands I commend My spirit"* (Lk. 23:46). In your suffering, entrust yourself to God.

The Indictment Of The Cross

In the Bible are astonishing words that will testify forever to the wickedness of man. Describing the execution of Jesus Christ, the gospel writers used the statement, "They crucified Him." Never before had One so innocent endured such an outpouring of human scorn and contempt. The whole process was a terrifying revelation of human sin.

First, there was the jealous hatred of the religious leaders of Israel. The Pharisees, Sadducees, and scribes joined forces to discredit Jesus (Mt. 22:15-46). They resented His popularity (Mt. 21:45-46; Jn. 12:19). They said His miracles were works of Satan (Mt. 12:22-30). They were appalled at His acceptance of ordinary people (Lk. 15:1-2). They hated His exposure of their hypocrisy (Mt. 15:1-14). Although they were looked up to as the spiritual leaders of Israel, they falsely accused, illegally tried, condemned, and crucified the One sent from God (Mt. 26–27).

Second, there was the greedy betrayal by Judas. As one of the disciples, he shared in the life and ministry of Jesus. The teachings, the miracles, the very heart and soul of the Savior were his to experience. But in the end, Judas chose to betray Him. As treasurer of the Twelve, he often stole from the common purse (Jn. 12:6). It is therefore no surprise that he would sell his own soul, and the Savior, for 30 pieces of silver (Mt. 26:14-16).

Third, there was the cunning cowardice of Pontius Pilate, the governor of Palestine appointed by Caesar. He was hated by the Jewish leaders. He knew they were manipulating him into killing Jesus, and he resisted it. All of his counter moves failed. Although he publicly proclaimed Christ's innocence, he did not set Him free. Giving in to pressure, he ordered the crucifixion of Christ.

Fourth, there is he fickle desire of the crowd. A few days earlier, the masses had cried, "Hosanna to the son of David," as Christ entered Jerusalem. But now they clamored for His death, shouting, "Crucify Him! Crucify Him!"

Fifth, there was the heartless cruelty of the Roman soldiers. They stripped Him and beat Him. They mocked Him. They spit on Him. They twisted a crown of thorns onto His head. They led Him away, bruised and bleeding, and crucified Him. What monstrous behavior!

Now, it would be easy for us to condemn these people. But let's be honest. Those wicked deeds against the innocent Son of God represent the truth about all of us. They are an indictment of our own sin.

The Call Of The Cross

Look again at the cross. Look at the One dying there. He never sinned, yet He is on the cross to bear the penalty for the sins of the whole world. He's dying there on your behalf. That should be you on that cross.

It's an ugly scene, isn't it? It shows us how terrible sin really is, and what a horrible price had to be paid to set us free from it. If you are a Christian, coming one more time to the cross should fill your heart with gratitude for what Christ did for you there. As your sacrifice and substitute, He made it possible for you to be forgiven and to be saved from your sin. Why don't you give Him your thanks right now? Then determine to walk in obedience to God.

> "God so loved the world that He gave His only begotten Son, that whoever believes in Him should not perish but have everlasting life."
> John 3:16

If you are not a Christian, won't you trust Him as your Savior? Your sin is real. You cannot do anything at all about it—except to trust in Jesus Christ. Don't wait. Tell Him that you believe in Him as your personal Savior. Ask Him to save you. He will, because it was for you that He died on that excruciating cross. He was your sacrifice. He paid the penalty for your sin. Trust Him now!

The Satisfaction Of The Cross

by Darlene Lehman as told to Judith Fabisch

If there was ever a time I didn't want to be accepted by God, I don't remember it. Our home was religious. Grandmother never had to force me to go to church on Sunday or Holy Days. After school, I often stopped at the cool, dimly lit cathedral near our house and knelt in one of the empty pews. It was a devotion of agony. I wanted God's forgiveness so badly, but He always seemed so very far away.

When I was about 10, the bishop visited our cathedral. While he was there, he blessed some holy water. Grandmother sent me to get a bottle of it to put in the small vials scattered around our home. I ran all the way to the cathedral, but I walked home much more slowly. I was thinking hard. I wanted so much to be accepted by God. Impulsively, I drank the holy water! Grandmother could not be angry with me, for she understood the guilt and desire that can be in a young girl's heart. But still I was not satisfied.

> "I begged God. I cried out to Him. I pleaded with Him to reveal Himself to me. And the answer finally came from an unexpected place."

High school did not remove the thirst that was in my soul, but I was soon occupied with studies, friends, and dating. Within a year of graduation I met and married Dick. It wasn't long before I was settled into the routine of establishing a home and family.

Although I loved my husband and my home, I longed more than ever for spiritual peace. I increased my acts of devotion to my church, attending faithfully and doing extra things to try to meet God's approval. But I still came away empty. I even went to an evangelistic meeting downtown. But I didn't understand what was being said, so I walked away frustrated. I was ready to do anything to please God.

I begged God. I cried out to Him. I pleaded with Him to reveal Himself to me. And the answer finally came from an unexpected place—through my mother-in-law. A sense of peace surrounded her, and she was always very kind. So when she asked me to attend a Christian women's club meeting with her, I was glad to go. A missionary was speaking. In clear, loving, unmistakable terms, she brought us to the cross. I understood for the first time the meaning of Christ's death—praise God! I realized that I should have come here—to the cross—a long time ago. I knew that the thirst of my soul would be satisfied here. I accepted the love and forgiveness of God. With tears of joy, I trusted Christ and His sacrifice for me.

The years have not been easy since. In time I left my church because of the emptiness of its ritual. I grew rapidly in Christ and in my commitment to Him. Dick didn't understand, and eventually he left me. But the Lord has sustained me and the children throughout the years.

The peace and satisfaction I found at the cross has been real—far greater than could ever be found in a bottle of holy water. The forgiveness of sins and acceptance by a holy God can be found only at the cross.

4

Did Christ Really
Rise From The Dead?

So much depends on the answer to this question. The reliability of the Bible. The answer to your search for meaning. The destiny of all people. It all depends on whether or not Jesus is alive. Did His body ever leave the tomb?

No matter which side of the issue you are on—a Christian who has faith in the resurrection or a nonbeliever who finds this miracle too good to be true—we hope this booklet will help you. Explore with us why we can trust the biblical account of what happened on that first Easter morning.

Dave Branon

Why Look Back?

Consider for a moment what mankind has accomplished. We've built spaceships that can leave our solar system. We've transplanted hearts into week-old babies. We've computerized everything from architecture to zoology. We've made tremendous progress in many areas of life.

Then why go backward? Why step 2,000 years into history to put our faith in an event that violates the laws of science? Why insist that the resurrection is anything more than a myth? After all, isn't DEAD MAN COMES ALIVE the kind of headline we usually expect to find on those tabloids that litter the supermarket checkout lanes?

Can educated, refined people living in the 21st century be convinced that Jesus really did come back from the dead? Many say no. They feel we have progressed too far to consider the resurrection of Jesus to be an authentic historical event. These skeptics say:

"Miracles are not scientific." To people of science, dead means dead. They have no evidence that anything that was dead ever came back to life spontaneously. Therefore, they aren't easily convinced that in one special case the normal processes of decay were halted. It goes against their established data to believe that a dead man came back to life.

"It was spiritual, not physical, resurrection." Some "enlightened" modern-day skeptics maintain that the disciples did not really see Jesus with their eyes; they "saw" Him with their hearts. They had a spiritual awakening because of Jesus' great sacrifice, and that spurred them on to preach about Him. Thus, He could be "resurrected" in the heart of anyone who accepted His teachings. To those who hold this view, Jesus was a great teacher whose ministry ended on the cross but whose influence continues through His words and philosophies.

"The biblical accounts are too contradictory." Some people think that if the Gospel writers could not agree on all the details, then we cannot be sure they got any part of the story straight. For instance, they point out that each of the four accounts of the morning scene at the tomb records a different number of women who were there. "A contemporary thinker," they say, "could never accept as evidence a story with such discrepancies."

"The historical accounts aren't trustworthy." Obviously, no reporters from the Jerusalem Star were at the garden on that resurrection morning to record the event. Therefore, the nonbiblical historical accounts we have concerning Jesus' resurrection were written some time after the event. To people who have grown accustomed to instantaneous news, that alone makes those accounts undependable.

So, the question remains. Can a technologically advanced society that continues to open new vistas of scientific knowledge believe in a miracle that 20 centuries of research have not been able to duplicate?

Fact Or Fiction?

Truth is not negotiable. Historical statements of fact are not open to question. When we read, for example, that George Washington and his men spent the winter of 1777 enduring wretched conditions at Valley Forge, we are obligated to believe it. Although none of us observed their long, deadly winter, what we know about it is supported by the written testimony of those who were there and by the scholarship of later inquirers who studied the Revolutionary War. The written accounts may differ on a few minor details, but we know that we can trust the record of the historians.

In a historical sense, the resurrection stands on ground that is just as solid as the story of George Washington's winter at Valley Forge. Reliable witnesses wrote about meeting and talking with Jesus after His death. Skeptical enemies noticed His disappearance from the tomb. Extrabiblical, historical reports were given of His resurrection. Eyewitnesses of Jesus' post-death appearances died defending their belief in it.

In order for an honest historian to be convinced that something actually happened, he needs to see

> "The Christian Savior had lived and associated with men whose minds and senses apprehended His person, acts, and character. These witnesses had transmitted their knowledge directly, and they had testified to the life of Jesus Christ and His teaching. Jesus was then a historical, not a mythical, being."
>
> Clifford Moore

two specific criteria met: (1) The event in question must be supported by the testimony of believable, trustworthy witnesses. And (2) the circumstantial evidence must be authentic. When both of these demands are clearly supported by the evidence at hand, the inquirer is compelled by logic to believe that the event actually took place. We will see that each of these criteria is met by the things we know about the resurrection.

Even so, some still don't believe. To make that refusal, a person must not only reject the eyewitness accounts and the circumstantial evidence, but he must make an even greater leap. The person who thinks that the resurrection is a fraud or a hoax must reject the entire New Testament. There can be no picking and choosing. If the resurrection is a hoax, then so is the New Testament and everything Jesus said or did. Claiming that Christ was a great teacher or a prophet—as even most unbelievers attest—while rejecting His resurrection is an impossible position. Consider what Jesus said during His ministry—before the crucifixion:

> *The Son of Man must suffer many things, and be rejected by the elders and chief priests and scribes, and be killed, and be raised the third day (Lk. 9:22).*

> *For as Jonah was three days and three nights in the belly of the great fish, so will the Son of Man be three days and three nights in the heart of the earth (Mt. 12:40).*

Think about it. Wouldn't we consider a man who made such wild claims to be untrustworthy if he couldn't follow through on his predictions? Instead of calling such a person a great teacher, wouldn't we call him a charlatan and a threat to mankind? There can be no middle ground. If Jesus did not do what He said He would do, He must be rejected completely. And along with Him go the Old Testament (because of its predictions of the Messiah's coming), the trustworthiness of Paul (who converted to Christ at the cost of beatings, imprisonments, and banishment from his former colleagues), and 2,000 years of church history (which rests solely on the resurrection).

> "It may be said that the historical evidence for the resurrection is stronger than for any other miracle anywhere narrated."
> William Lyon Phelps,
> Yale University

The evidence to be presented in the next few pages is based on the biblical and historical data as we know it. We will see why both secular and religious scholars find Jesus to be a captivating, historical person. So, let's get logical. Let's take a hard look at the evidence that gives us reason to believe that Jesus rose from the dead.

The Evidence For Christ's Resurrection

OBSERVATION 1:
THE VERIFICATION OF JESUS' DEATH

We have to start with the bad news. Jesus' confrontation with the religious leaders of Israel cost Him His

life. When the Roman soldiers removed Him from that awful cross of Golgotha, He was dead. As horrible as this fact is, the validity of the resurrection accounts hinges on it.

If, as some critics say, Jesus did no more than faint from the pain, there would be no need for a resurrection. For a person to be raised from the dead, he must first have died. To deny Christ's death, therefore, is to remove all possibility of resurrection. But the Bible teaches that He died.

In the four Gospel accounts of Jesus' crucifixion, His death is spoken of in two distinct terms. In

Matthew 27:50 and in John 19:30, the writers said He "yielded up" or "gave up" His spirit. The other accounts both record that He "breathed His last" (Mk. 15:37; Lk. 23:46).

Remarkably, Matthew, Mark, and Luke each recorded a simultaneous event that occurred some distance from Calvary. They wrote that as Jesus died, "the veil of the temple was torn in two from top to bottom" (Mk. 15:38). This miraculous event signaled the end of the Old Testament era of animal sacrifice and limited access to God. But that's not all it meant. It also verified Jesus' death, because it demonstrated that His complete sacrifice had satisfied God's demands. For centuries, God had required the death of an unblemished lamb as an atonement for sin. Now Jesus, the sinless Lamb of God, had become the new sacrifice. The veil was no longer needed, for access to God had been opened to all who would believe in Christ.

The following events at the site of the crucifixion help verify that Jesus was dead:

- The Roman soldiers did not break Jesus' legs, because they "saw that He was already dead" (Jn. 19:33).
- The soldiers plunged a spear into Jesus' side, and from it came both water and blood (Jn. 19:34). Medical experts say that if He were not already dead, this in itself would have killed Him. Others have concluded that the pouring out of water and blood from His side was proof that Jesus was no longer alive.

- When Joseph of Arimathea asked for the body of Christ so he and Nicodemus could bury Him, Pontius Pilate ordered a centurion to verify that Jesus was dead (Mk. 15:43-45). The Roman governor would not release the body to Joseph until the centurion was certain that all signs of life were gone. You can be sure that an officer in the Roman army would not make a mistake about an important matter like this in his report to such a high official as Pilate.

> "[Jesus] was crucified and died under Pontius Pilate. He really, and not merely in appearance, was crucified, and died, and in the sight of beings in heaven and on earth, and under the earth . . . . He also rose again in 3 days."
>
> Ignatius, second-century historian

- Joseph and Nicodemus prepared the body for burial according to Jewish custom. This included wrapping it "in a clean linen cloth" (Mt. 27:59), anointing the body with "a mixture of myrrh and aloes" (Jn. 19:39), and placing it "in a tomb which had been hewn out of the rock" (Mk. 15:46). It seems obvious that any sign of life would have been detected by these bereaved friends. Surely they would not have buried a breathing Jesus.

- The Pharisees and chief priests met with Pilate to discuss what had occurred. They made such remarks as "while He was still alive" (Mt. 27:63). Soldiers were ordered to secure the tomb with a seal. In addition, guards were placed on duty to prevent the disciples from coming to "steal Him away" (v.64). The Jewish leaders and the Roman authorities knew beyond a doubt that Jesus was dead.

OBSERVATION 2:
THE EMPTY TOMB

The Sabbath had ended, and Jesus' friends could now come to visit the tomb. As morning broke on the new day, the women who had watched Joseph

and Nicodemus bury Jesus came back to anoint His body. It was Sunday now—a somber day that, as far as the women knew, would be followed by many more days just like it. They were undoubtedly resigned to a future of sad pilgrimages such as this one. They knew of nothing else they could do for their fallen loved one but to grieve at His tomb and to put spices on His body. But what a surprise lay ahead!

As they walked toward the garden, they worried aloud about who could roll away the heavy stone so they could go inside the tomb and apply their spices. But when they arrived, they saw that the stone had already been moved! They were greeted by an angel, who told them that Jesus had risen.

With this background in mind, let's look at the evidence that the tomb was empty. First, we can depend on the historical record. Surely the authorities of Jesus' day wanted nothing more than to have Jesus stay where Joseph had put Him. The mere fact that they sealed the tomb and placed guards to protect it—a highly unusual act—indicated that they were determined to keep the body behind that stone barrier. Suppose they had been able to do that. You can be sure the Sanhedrin and other officials would have been the first to use the knowledge of an occupied tomb as evidence when the disciples began to announce to everyone that they had seen Jesus alive. Yet no historical evidence exists to suggest that those officials knew where the body was. As we will see, the evidence shows that it was no longer in the tomb.

> "The resurrection proclamation could not have been maintained in Jerusalem for a single day, for a single hour, if the emptiness of the tomb had not been established as a fact."
>
> Paul Althus

Second, there is something even more conclusive than the officials' inaction—the actions of several eyewitnesses. The first to see and report the empty tomb were the women with the spices. Mark's account sets the scene for us:

Entering the tomb, they saw a young man clothed in a long white robe sitting on the right side; and they were alarmed. But he said to them, "Do not be alarmed. You seek Jesus of Nazareth, who was crucified. He is risen! He is not here" (16:5-6).

John and Peter were the next to see that Jesus was gone. When they heard the unbelievably good news from Mary and the other women, they raced to the tomb. John got there first but didn't go in. Instead, he peered through the opening and saw the linen wrappings that Jesus had left behind. Characteristically, Peter was not content with a long-distance view. He charged right into the tomb and spied the linen wrappings and the face cloth lying undisturbed and neatly arranged. Then John entered and saw the wrappings. John, it should be noted, is the one who wrote this account as recorded in chapter 20 of his Gospel. If you need an eyewitness to convince you that the tomb was empty, you have one in the apostle John. He was there, and he wrote down what he saw. That is solid historical evidence in anyone's book.

> If you need an eyewitness to convince you that the tomb was empty, you have one in John.

A third strong piece of evidence that the tomb was empty is the reaction of the authorities when the guards reported the events in the garden. They wanted to destroy the credibility and influence of Jesus. Therefore, they would surely have been foolish to spread the rumor that the disciples had stolen the body—if Jesus were still in the tomb. No, Jesus' disappearance was the sole cause for their concern. Surely their collusion with the guards is solid proof that there was no body in the tomb.

We are faced with two facts. (1) Jesus died and was buried. (2) In a short time, His tomb became empty. The question remains: Where was Jesus?

OBSERVATION 3:
THE APPEARANCES OF JESUS

Jesus' friends weren't looking for what they were about to see. Although they had heard and closely followed

Jesus' teaching for 3 years, they just never fully understood that He was going to rise from the dead. Therefore, they would have had no reason to make up stories in which they claimed to have seen Him. To them, that wasn't even an option. Sure, they missed Jesus. And just as anyone who has lost a loved one or friend longs to see him, so also they had the desire to see Jesus. But they did not expect that they ever would (see Jn. 20:9).

Yet see Him they did! First at the tomb. Then on the dusty Emmaus road. Then in the upper room.

Over and over, in different settings, Jesus appeared to His friends. For 40 days He made His presence known throughout the land. Let's look at who saw Jesus and where He appeared. It's one more piece of evidence for the resurrection.

To Mary Magdalene At The Tomb (Jn. 20:11-18). Mary had been standing outside the empty tomb crying because, as she said, "They have taken away my Lord, and I do not know where they have laid Him" (v.13). His death, combined with her fear that His body had been stolen, had engulfed her in heart-wrenching despair. But when Jesus startled her into recognizing Him by calling out, "Mary!" she rushed to Him in joy and relief. Then she ran to tell the disciples that she had seen the Lord.

To Several Women As They Ran From The Tomb (Mt. 28:9-10). These women had already heard that Jesus was alive, even though they had not yet seen Him. They had just left the tomb, where an angel had told them that Jesus had "risen from the dead." When they saw the Lord, they "held Him by the feet and worshiped Him" (v.9). Jesus told them to spread the news that He was alive and to tell the disciples to meet Him in Galilee.

To Two Disciples On The Emmaus Road (Lk. 24:13-32). Imagine the drama of this scene. Two disciples were walking the 7 dusty miles from Jerusalem to Emmaus when a fellow traveler caught up with them and struck up a conversation, asking what they were talking about. Apparently, they had been discussing the death and entombment of Jesus, because they were surprised that the stranger wasn't familiar with their topic.

They said, in effect, "Do you mean to say that you don't know about Jesus' death?" The two then explained why they were so sad—that though some women had seen the empty tomb and claimed that Jesus was alive, they had not yet seen Him. These disciples would not believe without seeing the evidence for themselves.

An exciting surprise awaited the pair when they arrived at Emmaus. The three of them stopped to eat, and as they ate, the disciples' "eyes were opened" and they recognized that this mysterious stranger was Jesus. But before they could speak again, He "vanished from their sight" (v.31).

To Peter At An Unknown Location (Lk. 24:33-35). In this passage, we are not given a direct look at the meeting between Peter and Jesus. All we know is that when the disciples who had been to Emmaus returned, they learned that Peter had seen the Lord too. Imagine the excitement that must have been generated in that place!

To 10 Disciples In The Upper Room (Lk. 24:36-43). Suddenly this praise meeting of the disciples was interrupted. As they sat comparing notes about the thrilling reality of seeing Jesus, He suddenly appeared. As might be expected, the men were startled because they thought they were seeing a spirit (v.37). Jesus quickly laid that idea to rest by offering to have them touch His hands and feet, and by eating supper with them.

To 11 Disciples In The Upper Room (Jn. 20:26-31). It must have been a long week for Thomas. The other 10 disciples had met with Jesus in the upper room, but he had not. Surely they had spent time trying to convince Thomas that they really had seen Jesus. But he reacted the same way they had when they heard from the women who first saw Jesus. They were not convinced without hard evidence, and Thomas wanted the same advantage. Now he was about to get it. Jesus suddenly appeared to the men and said to Thomas, "Reach your finger here, and look at My hands" (v.27). Then Thomas believed, exclaiming, "My Lord and my God!" (v.28).

To Seven Men At The Sea Of Galilee (Jn. 21:1-25). Things had begun to return to normal for the disciples. They had gone back to work. Some went on an all-night fishing trip on the Sea of Galilee. But the fish weren't cooperating, and the men had an empty boat. As daylight broke over the water, they saw a man standing on the shore, shouting advice to them. The seven seamen did what He suggested and nearly capsized their boat with all the fish they dragged ashore.

When John informed Peter, "It is the Lord!" (Jn. 21:7), Peter jumped in and swam to shore. When they all arrived on the beach, they saw that Jesus had prepared a hot breakfast of fish and bread for them. Jesus then offered to cook a few of the fish they had just caught.

To 11 Disciples On A Mountain (Mt. 28:16-20). This is the first planned meeting between the disciples and Jesus recorded after the resurrection. Matthew wrote that the disciples proceeded "into Galilee, to the mountain which Jesus had appointed for them" (28:16). There He met with the Eleven, and probably some others. Perhaps this included the "500 brethren" mentioned in 1 Corinthians 15:6.

What is significant is that even though the Eleven worshiped Jesus when they saw Him, "some doubted" (Mt. 28:17). Although it is possible that a few of these men were still doubting Jesus' resurrection, it is more probable that the skeptics were disciples who didn't have the advantage of touching Jesus and eating with Him. They would naturally have been more hesitant to believe that this was the same man who had been crucified a few weeks before. Yet the fact that doubters are mentioned shows that the disciple who wrote the account was not afraid to talk about the skepticism of some of the observers.

To His Disciples Near Bethany (Acts 1:9-12). The final appearance of Jesus to His disciples ended with His disappearance. As He stood talking with them about the command He had just given them to be His witnesses, "He was taken up, and a cloud received Him out of their sight" (v.9). This turned out to be a commencement of sorts for the disciples. Just a few weeks earlier, they had been a disheartened group whose leader was dead. Now they were enthusiastic evangelists. They "returned to Jerusalem with great joy" (Lk. 24:52), and "they went out and preached everywhere" (Mk. 16:20).

The evidence was clear. Jesus was alive. Now their job was to go and tell people about it.

OBSERVATION 4:
THE REACTION OF THE JEWISH OFFICIALS
A Roman soldier was no coward. He was a specially trained, tough-minded, well-equipped warrior. But notice the reaction of the soldiers who were protecting Jesus' tomb when they felt the earth move and saw an

angel roll back the stone (Mt. 28:2). They "shook for fear of him, and became like dead men" (v.4).

They probably realized that they had more to be afraid of than an angel. Their training told them that keeping watch was an important commission. They knew that various punishments were handed out to soldiers who couldn't stay awake on guard duty. Sometimes they were beaten; other times they were set afire. Most of the time they were executed. These brave, well-armed men had no way to stop the angel, so they had double reason to be afraid.

But look what they did next. They turned themselves in! Facing sure punishment, they still felt that they must report this amazing event to their superiors. Once they had spilled their story to the chief priests and elders, their fears turned to relief. The officials, realizing that sending Jesus to His death had not accomplished their purpose, decided to concoct a story. They bribed the soldiers to spread the news that "His disciples came at night and stole Him away while we slept" (v.13).

The soldiers must have done what they were told, for Matthew commented that the story begun by those chief priests was "commonly reported among the Jews until this day" (v.15). Devised in the face of the fact of the resurrection, this fabrication stayed alive for many years among those who refused to believe that Jesus had risen.

It wouldn't have taken much effort to refute their story. First, if the disciples had indeed been able to steal the body of Jesus, how would the guards have known that it was they who had stolen it? Didn't the story go, "while we slept"? Second, it seems preposterous that a group of men could have sneaked up on highly trained, albeit slumbering, soldiers without waking them. And then to think that they could have moved the stone, unwrapped 100 pounds of graveclothes, folded them neatly, lifted the body, and carried it away while the soldiers slept is even more ridiculous.

Yes, the officials knew that Jesus had risen. Their reaction proves it. Their bribe verifies it. And their hastily concocted story authenticates it.

OBSERVATION 5:
THE OUTLOOK OF JESUS' DISCIPLES

Sometimes you have to wonder about the disciples. They certainly didn't seem to be the kind of men you would recruit if you wanted to promote a revolutionary concept.

For instance, when Jesus tried to explain to them what would happen in the days ahead, they often misunderstood. When He asked some of them to stay with Him during His all-night prayer vigil, they kept falling asleep. When He talked of servanthood, they argued about their own greatness. When He tried to tell them that He would be raised up after 3 days, they didn't get it.

On the night Jesus was arrested, the disciples ran for their lives. Peter couldn't even stand up to a servant girl when she identified him as a friend of Jesus. The disciples just didn't seem like the men of action you would need if you wanted to win a following and influence the world.

But something happened to change all that. What would change a cowardly group of mourners into a courageous band of evangelists who were willing to stand up and testify that the crucified Jesus was alive? What changed them into willing martyrs for their faith?

> "Nothing less than a witness as awesome as the resurrected Christ could have caused those men to maintain to their dying whispers that Jesus is alive."
>
> Charles Colson

Some would say that the disciples had nothing stronger to spur them on than a story they had made up. But can you imagine what it would take to believe this? Just picture Peter standing up before the disciples, who had remained safely hidden behind locked doors after Jesus' death for fear of their lives, and saying, "Well, the entire weight of the Roman government was just used to put Jesus to death by crucifixion. Even though He is still dead, we are going to start a rumor that He isn't. We are going to say that He rose from the tomb and that we all saw Him."

Did they make up the story? If so, why would they later risk their lives for nothing? If they hadn't even understood for sure that Jesus planned to rise from the dead, why would they break out of their anonymity with such a far-fetched scheme? And why would they record their fabrication in the Gospel accounts, complete with details?

A fictional story can't possibly account for the changes in the disciples. Take, for instance, the transformation of Thomas. Of all the disciples, he seemed the least likely to be convinced. His pessimism was first revealed earlier, when Jesus mentioned His plans to go to Bethany where Lazarus had just died. Thomas had suggested to his fellow disciples, "Let us also go, that we may die with Him" (Jn. 11:16). Although this statement suggests a degree of courage, it also implies that Thomas was resigned to martyrdom. If that was his typical response, it is no wonder he responded to the disciples' claim that they had seen Jesus after His death by saying, "Unless I see . . . I will not believe" (Jn. 20:25). Does this sound like someone who is willing to rekindle the anger of the Roman officials by claiming that Jesus was alive if He really wasn't?

Now look at Thomas a week later. In the upper room, surrounded by his 10 friends who had already seen Jesus, he saw the Savior face to face. Finally, Thomas was convinced. His statement "My Lord and my God!" (Jn. 20:28) is the ultimate proclamation of belief in Jesus' resurrection. Here was victory that could be won only through hard evidence. It's the only thing that could have changed this skeptic into a believer.

No, the disciples were not the type of men who could have lived a lie as far-reaching as one that claimed a dead man wasn't dead anymore. They might have misunderstood Jesus on occasion, but they were basically honest men. They had no reason to devise such a scheme, and they didn't have the courage it would take to defend such a bald-faced lie. Peter would never have been hanged upside down for a trumped-up story. Mark would not have been dragged through the streets to his death if he had been defending fiction. James would not have been beheaded for a falsehood. Thomas wouldn't have been pierced with a lance for a lie. Yet tradition says that these men died the horrible deaths just described. What a testimony to the truth of their claims! They were willing to die for the One who overcame death for them—and for us!

OBSERVATION 6:
THE START OF THE CHRISTIAN CHURCH

The Christian church was not born nor does it exist today on the basis of Jesus' life and teachings. The church that began less than 2 months after Jesus' death is the result of something more significant than His great sayings, parables, and philosophies. It began because a group of people in Jerusalem testified that they saw Jesus alive after He had been killed. Without the faith of those resurrection witnesses and the new faith of those who believed their testimony about it, there would be no Christian church today.

Let's see what the people were told when they were first given the opportunity to embrace this new faith. This will help us to see what caused the church to take hold in the first century.

Standing before people from all over the Roman Empire, including many from Jerusalem, Peter described Jesus as the One "God raised up" (Acts 2:24). He also said, "This Jesus God has raised up, of which we are all witnesses" (v.32). As a result of this clear, straightforward message, 3,000 people believed Peter and were baptized that very day.

In a later sermon, this man who had earlier denied that he knew Jesus now called Him the "Prince of life, whom God raised from the dead" (Acts 3:15). After hearing of Peter's testimony, the rulers and priests in Jerusalem put him on trial. Even when he faced the wrath of the religious leaders, Peter stood by his story that "the God of our fathers raised up Jesus whom you murdered by hanging on a tree" (Acts 5:30).

These are the kinds of statements that led to the start of the church. No one could hedge on the reason for Peter's fervor. He was not preaching a creed nor advocating a philosophy. He was telling people that the crucified Christ was alive. That was the essence of his message. And that was the only message the Christian church needed to catch fire. For 2,000 years, it's been the driving force behind the church.

OBSERVATION 7:
THE EXPECTATION OF CHRIST'S RETURN

One of the most important activities of the early church was to share in what we now call the communion service. It was a time to remember Jesus' death and to reflect on His sacrifice. It was a time of celebration. But what would the early Christian have had to celebrate if Jesus were still dead? These people were living in Jesus' generation. They would have known if the

resurrection story were not true. Yet they listened and obeyed when Paul said:

As often as you eat this bread and drink this cup, you proclaim the Lord's death till He comes (1 Cor. 11:26).

This verse makes it obvious that the first-century believers were eagerly awaiting Jesus' return. They could not have believed in His second coming without first knowing that He was alive. Otherwise, how would He be able to come back?

This idea that Jesus would return to be with His people again was taught throughout the New Testament. Jesus Himself taught it when He said:

I will come again and receive you to Myself; that where I am, there you may be also (Jn. 14:3).

Paul emphasized the same theme when he said:

Our citizenship is in heaven, from which we also eagerly wait for the Savior, the Lord Jesus Christ (Phil. 3:20).

And John said:

Behold, He is coming with clouds, and every eye will see Him (Rev. 1:7).

Without the resurrection, these claims would all be useless, frivolous, unfounded lies. No one would dare predict such an event as Jesus' return if He were in fact lying in a tomb, or if His body had been taken away and hidden. No, John and Paul knew exactly what had transpired on that resurrection day. What would have been the purpose of telling about His return if they were harboring the knowledge of a dead Jesus?

What The Opposition Says

A premise that cannot stand up against opposing views is not worthy of our trust. Therefore, it is only fair that we mention some of the theories that have been proposed to explain away the resurrection. Looking carefully at the logic of these ideas, we will be able to see how they fare when stacked up against the evidence already presented.

THEORY: The body was stolen from the tomb. In this theory, the disciples are the culprits. They sneaked up to the stone, rolled it away, and walked off with Jesus' body. That's why it wasn't there when the women, John, and Peter arrived at the tomb on the first day of the week.

OBJECTIONS: Why would the disciples want Jesus' body? Who was it who appeared to all those people later? How did the disciples sneak past the guards? Why would an angel lie about the reason for the tomb being empty?

THEORY: The authorities took the body. Knowing that the disciples had an unusual interest in Jesus, the authorities—both governmental and religious—made sure they would not see Him again. They opened the tomb and took the body.

OBJECTIONS: Why didn't the authorities produce it to disprove the claims of Peter and others just a few weeks later? What turned the disheartened disciples into fiery proponents of a new cause if they had not seen Jesus again?

THEORY: Jesus' friends went to the wrong tomb. It had been a terrifying week for the disciples and the others who had grown so close to Jesus. Therefore they became disoriented and went to the wrong grave. That's why they found an empty tomb.

OBJECTIONS: Whose graveclothes did John and Peter find? What was an angel doing at someone else's gravesite? Is it possible that they all forgot their directions at the same time?

THEORY: Jesus only fainted. This theory says that Jesus didn't die on the cross. Instead, He fell into a deep swoon. Then, when He was placed in the tomb, He was revived by the cool, damp air. That explains His later appearances.

OBJECTIONS: What caused the soldiers to misinterpret the evidence and certify that Jesus was dead? Why didn't Joseph notice that Jesus wasn't dead when he wrapped Him in linen? How did Jesus, who had been nearly dead just days before, push away the stone and walk about town in perfectly good health?

THEORY: Jesus' friends saw hallucinations. The resurrection makes a nice story, says this theory, but the disciples never saw any of the things they thought they saw. In fact, some say, they hallucinated, seeing images in their minds that corresponded with what they wanted to see.

OBJECTIONS: Is there evidence that suggests that 11 people can hallucinate the same image? How about 500 simultaneous, identical hallucinations? Can people drag out hallucinations over 7 weeks, in many locations, and under various circumstances?

All The Savior's Men

Former presidential counsel Charles Colson tells how his Watergate experience can be used to support the testimony of the first-century men who said they saw the resurrected Jesus.

How do we know that Jesus was resurrected? We have the eyewitness accounts of the 11 apostles who were with Him and, of course, the apostle Paul who saw Him. They were with Him before His crucifixion and for the 40 days between His resurrection and His ascension. They lived for as long as 40 years thereafter, never once denying that they had seen Jesus raised from the dead.

What does that have to do with Watergate? I'll tell you. In June 1972, I was home on a weekend with my wife and children. We had a few days off because President Nixon was in Key Biscayne, Florida. My phone that was connected to the White House rang. It was John Erlichmann. He told me that some burglars had broken into the Democratic National Headquarters in Washington. I started laughing hysterically because I thought to myself, "Of all the ridiculous places for anybody to break into in Washington, DC."

I went away from that phone call shaking my head and feeling a little despair. I thought, "Now we have a campaign issue, but it will go away after the election." Well, as you know, it didn't!

The log showed that in the months immediately following the 1972 election, I was with President Nixon more than any other aide. Watergate never came up. We first started to discuss it in February 1973, when the Ervin hearings started. On March 21,

1973, John Dean walked into the Oval Office and said, "Mr. President, there is a cancer growing on your presidency." That's the first time the President really knew there was a conspiracy in the White House. That's the first time it became a criminal act inside the White House.

John Dean's memoirs record that 3 days after that meeting in the Oval Office he began to get nervous about his own role. That's when he hired a lawyer. On April 8, Dean went to the prosecutors to bargain for immunity so that he would not be prosecuted. In turn, he would testify against the President. Later, he said, "I did it to save my own skin." When he went to the prosecutors to bargain for immunity, it was all over.

Then the other aides started to go in. I took a lie detector test, and my lawyers leaked it to the *New York Times*. Everybody started to scramble for cover. The Watergate coverup was actually over because Mr. Nixon's presidency was doomed. Now, if you stop and figure it out, you will see that the Watergate coverup actually lasted 3 weeks or less—from March 21 to April 8, 1973.

Now put yourself in our position. Here we were, the 12 most powerful men in the United States. All the power of government was at our fingertips, but we could not keep a lie together for 3 weeks. The most powerful men in the world could not hold on to a lie. So weak is man that we couldn't do it.

> "Here we were, the 12 most powerful men in the United States. All the power of government was at our fingertips, but we could not keep a lie together for 3 weeks."
> Charles Colson

Are you going to tell me that those powerless apostles who were outcasts in their own land could be stoned, persecuted, and beaten, some for 40 years, never once denying that Jesus was raised from the dead? Impossible, humanly impossible—unless they had seen the risen Christ face to face. Otherwise, the apostle Peter would have been just another John Dean. He'd have gone in to turn state's evidence. He had already done it three times.

Is it likely, then, that a deliberate coverup, a plot to perpetuate a lie about the resurrection, could have survived the persecution of the apostles and the purge of the first-century believers who were cast by the thousands to the lions for refusing to renounce Christ? Is it not probable that at least one apostle would have "confessed" rather than being beheaded or stoned? Is it not likely that some "smoking gun" document might have been produced exposing the "Passover plot"? Surely one of the conspirators would have made a deal.

If Jesus was raised from the dead, as I am absolutely, intellectually positive that He was—and the evidence of history is overwhelming—it's not only a matter of faith but a matter of deepest intellectual conviction.

Taken from a speech by Charles Colson and from his book *Loving God*, Zondervan, ©1983.

Why Is This So Important?

Think of the key world events of the last couple of decades. The fall of the Berlin Wall. The Persian Gulf War. The conflict in Bosnia. The El Niño weather events. The terrorist destruction of New York's Twin Towers and attack on the Pentagon.

Or go back to an earlier era. Watergate. The oil crisis of the 70s. The Vietnam War. Man landing on the moon. Perhaps you've been around long enough to recall the assassination of President Kennedy. Hiroshima. The Holocaust. Pearl Harbor. Whatever comes to mind, you can be sure of this: No event in the last 100 years has affected every human on earth—no matter where he or she lives.

> "If Jesus is, as the resurrection asserts, God Himself who has come to our rescue, then to reject Him, or even to neglect Him, is sheer folly. That is why Jesus is not, never has been, and never can be just one among the religious leaders of mankind."
>
> Michael Green

Now think back through history. The Civil War. The Fall of the Bastille. The American Revolution. The discovery of the New World. The invention of the printing press. The signing of the Magna Carta. The Battle of Hastings. The Fall of the Roman Empire. Each of these events had extraordinary historical significance. But none of them has the kind of monumental, worldwide, eternal effects that one event almost 2,000 years ago claims to have. This event? The resurrection of Jesus Christ.

The Bible says that God came to earth as a man to pay the penalty of death for the sins of the world (Jn. 1:1-29; Rom. 6:23). But the Bible also says that if Jesus did not overpower death's grip to escape that cold, rocky tomb, He would not be able to provide us with victory over death (1 Cor. 15:12-19).

The implications of the resurrection of Jesus Christ must be considered honestly. Everything depends on it. Here is what Paul said:

> *[God] commands all men everywhere to repent, because He has appointed a day on which He will judge the world in righteousness by the Man whom He has ordained. He has given assurance of this to all by raising Him from the dead (Acts 17:30-31).*

According to the Bible, the eternal destiny of every human is at stake. Because of what Jesus did, each of us has two choices. We can live forever under God's blessing in heaven, or we can be separated from Him eternally in the torment of hell. It all depends on our response to Jesus' resurrection.

Our destiny is in God's hands. He alone must be satisfied. Not scientists. Not philosophers. Not educators. That's why what you believe about the resurrection is a matter of eternal life or eternal death.

It's Your Decision

Perhaps the most tense moment in a courtroom trial is the reading of the verdict. The judge calls on the jury foreman as he stands nervously before the jury, the judge, the gallery, the lawyers, and the defendant. No sound is heard except the wrinkle of paper as he unfolds the jury's decision. With hesitation in his voice, he reveals to the breathless crowd the fate of the accused.

After reading the evidence in this book, you too stand ready for a decision. But the Judge who awaits your choice is not a fellow human who has worked his way to the bench. The One who wants to know your decision has the authority to sentence you to an eternity of confinement in a prison called hell. Why? You are the defendant. You have been charged with sin (Rom. 3:23), and you face a sentence that is irreversible (Rom. 6:23). But here's the switch. You are also the jury. You get to make the decision based on the evidence.

So now it is time to make your decision. Do you believe that Jesus died as a sacrifice for your sins? Do you believe that He rose from that garden tomb to prove His deity and to establish Himself as the only mediator between God and you?

It's your choice. You've read the evidence. You've seen the historicity of the Bible's claims. Are you ready to put your faith in Jesus? Are you willing to accept His gift to you? He is waiting for your answer.

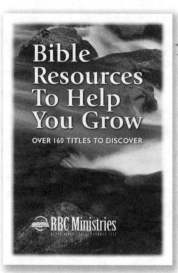